Vivian Wright
3 May 1968

D0893630

THOMAS HARDY AND HIS READERS

A Selection of Contemporary Reviews

THOMAS HARDY
and his readers

A Selection of
Contemporary Reviews

Edited
with a Commentary by
LAURENCE LERNER
and
JOHN HOLMSTROM

THE BODLEY HEAD

LONDON SYDNEY
TORONTO

Acknowledgements are due to the following for permission to include copyright material:

Miss Irene Cooper-Willis and the Trustees of the Hardy Estate for the material by Thomas Hardy

Miss Jennifer Gosse and Miss Sylvia Gosse for the review of *Jude* by Edmund Gosse

Macmillan & Co, Ltd for John Morley's report on *Under the Greenwood Tree*

John Murray, Ltd for an extract by W. H. Mallock in *The Quarterly Review*

The Society of Authors (as literary representative of the estate of Sir William Watson) for the review of *Tess* in *The Academy*

© Laurence Lerner and John Holmstrom, 1968
SBN 370 00461 2
Printed and bound in Great Britain for
The Bodley Head Ltd
9 Bow Street, London, WC2
by William Clowes & Sons Ltd, Beccles
Set in Monotype Scotch Roman No. 1
First published 1968

CONTENTS

8 · JUDE THE OBSCURE

9 · GENERAL APPRAISALS

Preface

This anthology of criticism is intended to show what contemporaries thought of the novels of Thomas Hardy. The world is full, nowadays, of critical anthologies which offer us a range of interpretations of the great writers of the past, by the great critics of the present: such books serve many functions, but the one thing they do not tell us, in their wealth of subtle, profound and ingenious commentary, is what impression the writers made on the readers for whom they were, in the first place, writing. Hardy may, in a sense, have been writing for Lionel Trilling and William Empson all the time; but, in another and more obvious sense, he was writing for the readers of the *Cornhill Magazine*, in which *Far from the Madding Crowd* first appeared.

This volume tells of two things: of the novels, and of the impression they made. It therefore has a double interest. It has the interest of all literary criticism, illuminating the books discussed, relating them to the critic's own experience of life; and an historical interest, showing us what the Victorians looked for in their favourite novelists. As far as the first (critical) interest is concerned, some of the critics are obviously worth more than others. Few reviewers are as penetrating as Edmund Gosse was on Hardy (or Sidney Colvin on George Eliot), and some of those included— but not many—are quite worthless. These latter are there for their historical interest, for our picture of the Victorian response is incomplete if it includes only the intelligent critics. Yet in another, and perhaps more genuine, sense of 'historical', a true historical reconstruction ought to pay particular attention to the best: Gosse speaks more truly for what readers were really thinking—or groping towards thinking—in the 1890s than do most of the everyday reviewers. These two approaches, critical and historical, are easily distinguished in theory, but almost impossible to disentangle in practice. Few readers of this volume will be interested in one without any touch of the other; and it goes without saying that even the most historically minded reader will get little from the critics if he has never read the novelist.

If all the novels had been given equal treatment, we would either have had to sacrifice full treatment of any, or else make the volume impossibly long. After a brief mention of *Desperate Remedies*, his first novel, we confine ourselves to the seven which stand out by common consent, and from these we have chosen three for full treatment: *Far from the Madding Crowd*, the first real success, and always one of his most popular; *Tess of the D'Urbervilles*, possibly his masterpiece; and the notorious *Jude the Obscure*, his last novel, whose hostile reception is so well known. Much more briefly, we have noticed *Under the Greenwood Tree*, *The Return of the Native*, *The Mayor of Casterbridge* and *The Woodlanders*.

The main source of material has been the daily, weekly and quarterly papers published in England, and these we have combed as thoroughly as we could. When we found interesting material elsewhere, we have included it. Each section contains a short note on the publishing history of the novel; then the reviews; then an editorial commentary. The general section at the end is taken both from articles on Hardy's work as a whole, and also from generalising digressions in the reviews. The authors of unsigned reviews, when we have been able to identify these, are named in brackets. We have had to decide what makes a review contemporary. The natural meaning might seem to be 'during the author's life', but for Hardy's novels this would be absurd. He lived for 33 years after the publication of *Jude the Obscure* and was a classic of the English novel long before he died. The end of his career as a novelist therefore makes a more appropriate terminus, but we have interpreted the formula loosely. The latest item is actually dated 1904.

Four books on Hardy have been very useful to us: F. E. Hardy's *Life*; Carl J. Weber's *Hardy in America*; and the bibliographies of Carl J. Weber (*The First Hundred Years of Thomas Hardy*) and R. L. Purdy (*Hardy: A Bibliographical Study*). Much of the material by Hardy which we have printed is now available in *Thomas Hardy's Personal Writings*, edited by Harold Orel. We owe thanks to the following for their help in tracing material or identifying anonymous reviews: Mr Charles Seaton of *The Spectator*, Mr Adrian Peasgood of the University of Sussex library, and Mlle Françoise Weil of the Bibliothèque Universitaire, Dijon.

Biographical Note

Thomas Hardy was born 2 June 1840 at Upper Bockhampton, near Dorchester. In 1856 he was articled to a local architect, and in 1862 went to London, where he stayed five years. After his return to Dorchester in 1867, he gradually gave up architecture for writing. He married Emma Gifford in 1874: the sad spoiling of their marriage is recorded in the poems he wrote after Emma's death in 1912. In 1914 he married Florence Emily Dugdale, who published the two memoirs that are still the main (almost the sole) sources for his life, *The Early Life of Thomas Hardy* (1928) and *The Later Years* (1930): these books contain copious extracts from his letters and notebooks and were virtually written by Hardy himself, as a kind of vicarious autobiography. Hardy's literary career forms a kind of sandwich. In his youth he wrote, but did not publish, a lot of poetry; his career as a novelist lasted from 1871 to 1896; and he then turned to poetry again, and wrote and published steadily until his death in 1928.

His novels, with dates of first publication in England in book form:

1871	*Desperate Remedies*
1872	*Under the Greenwood Tree*
1873	*A Pair of Blue Eyes*
1874	*Far from the Madding Crowd*
1876	*The Hand of Ethelberta*
1878	*The Return of the Native*
1880	*The Trumpet-Major*
1881	*A Laodicean*
1882	*Two on a Tower*
1886	*The Mayor of Casterbridge*
1887	*The Woodlanders*
1888	*Wessex Tales*
1891	*A Group of Noble Dames*
1891	*Tess of the D'Urbervilles*
1894	*Life's Little Ironies*
1896	*Jude the Obscure*

Two volumes that appeared after *Jude* were reprints of work
that had appeared in periodicals:

    1897   *The Well-Beloved*
    1913   *A Changed Man, The Waiting Supper, and other*
             Tales

1 · DESPERATE REMEDIES

⁋ *Desperate Remedies* was the second novel Hardy wrote, and the first he published. It was begun in the autumn of 1869, and most of it was finished by March 1870. The final (altered) version was done by the autumn of that year, and it was published on 25 March 1871 by Tinsley Brothers, partly at Hardy's own expense: he was required to contribute £75, and when the last copies were remaindered, he received £59 12s. 9d. back as his share. An American edition was published by Henry Holt in 1874.

The Athenaeum, 1 April 1871

'Desperate Remedies,' though in some respects an unpleasant story, is undoubtedly a very powerful one. We cannot decide, satisfactorily to our own mind, on the sex of the author; for while certain evidence, such as the close acquaintance which he or she appears (and, as far as we can judge, with reason) to possess with the mysteries of the female toilette, would appear to point to its being the work of one of that sex, on the other hand there are certain expressions to be met with in the book so remarkably coarse as to render it almost impossible that it should have come from the pen of an English lady. Yet, again, all the best anonymous novels of the last twenty years—a dozen instances will at once suggest themselves to the novel-reader—have been the work of female writers. In this conflict of evidence, we will confine ourselves to the inexpressive 'he' in speaking of our present author, if we chance to need a pronoun.

As to the story itself, it is, as we have said, disagreeable, inasmuch as it is full of crimes, in the discovery of which lies the main interest of the tale. We will not particularize them, as to do so would be to reveal the whole plot; but we may say that they are never purposeless, and that their revelation comes upon us step by step, and is worked out with considerable artistic power. The construction of the story is very curious. The various periods are accurately marked out in the headings of the chapters, and the sections into which they are divided. We have, for instance, 'Chapter III. The events of five days,' and this will be sub-divided into '§ 1. November the twenty-ninth,' '§ 2. From November the twenty-ninth to December the second,' and so throughout. If carefully carried out, as it is in the present book, this gives an air of reality which is far more satisfactory than the popular mottoes from some book of quotation which form the headings of chapters in nine-tenths of novels, though at the same time it may easily become an affectation.

The characters are often exceedingly good. The parish clerk, 'a sort of Bowdlerized rake,' who refers to the time 'before he took orders,' is really almost worthy of George Eliot, and so is the whole cider-making scene at the end of the first volume. The west-country dialect is also very well managed, without being a caricature. Occasionally, too, we come across a very happy hit—as, for instance, the allusion to 'the latent feeling which is rather common in these days among the unappreciated that, because some markedly successful men are fools, all markedly unsuccessful men are geniuses'; and the like.

There are a few faults of style and grammar, but very few. 'Whomsoever's' is an odd formation, and 'factitiously pervasive' is a clumsy expression. A lawyer, too, might find fault with a deed full of stops, and containing the phrase 'on the determination of this demise,' and a surgeon with '*os femoris*,' but these technical errors are few. On the whole, the chief blemish of the book will be found in the occasional coarseness to which we have alluded, and which we can hardly further particularize, but which, startling as it once or twice is, is confined wholly to expressions, and does not affect the main character of the story. If the author will purge himself of this, though even this is better than the prurient sentimentality with which we are so often nauseated, we see no reason why he should not write novels only a little, if at all, inferior to the best of the present generation.

❡ *Desperate Remedies* is almost unread nowadays. It is a thriller of considerable ingenuity and no plausibility whatever, with very little of the later Hardy in it: the parish clerk and the hero's father faintly anticipate the more famous choruses of rustics, and the incredible windings of plot occasionally have an ironic quality that is recognisable Hardy. There are even a few unmistakably sardonic touches, such as this reflection of a man about to die:

'I am now about to enter on my normal condition. For people are almost always in their graves. When we survey the long race of men, it is strange and still more strange to find that they are mainly dead men, who have scarcely ever been otherwise.'

But nothing of importance in the book either anticipates the later novels, or suggests a writer of genius. The review therefore has little critical interest, and is included to show the beginning of Hardy's career. It was the first review he ever received; together with three others, it was pasted in his scrap-book, and kept.

One of the others was the hostile notice in *The Spectator*, which called it 'a desperate remedy for an emaciated purse'. Florence Emily Hardy's *Life* records his first reaction to this attack:

'He remembered, for long years after, how he had read this review as he sat on a stile leading to the ewelease he had to cross on his way home to Bockhampton. The bitterness of that moment was never forgotten; at the time he wished that he were dead.'

His friend Moule told him not to mind, and himself reviewed the book favourably in *The Saturday Review*: Moule's review of *Under the Greenwood Tree*, in the same paper, is given below.

2 · UNDER
THE GREENWOOD TREE

❧ Hardy's first novel was called *The Poor Man and the Lady*. It was sent to Macmillan, and drew a long letter of advice from Alexander Macmillan to the author. 'Your description of country life among working men is admirable,' Macmillan wrote; but he was critical of the conversation 'in drawing rooms and ballrooms ... Nothing could justify such a wholesale blackening of a class but large and intimate knowledge of it.' Macmillan compared the book with Thackeray, who 'makes them not greatly better in many respects, but ... he meant fun, you "*mean mischief*".' Hardy re-wrote the book to meet some of these suggestions, but it was in the end rejected.

The Poor Man and the Lady has ceased to exist; but after *Desperate Remedies* had been published, Hardy set to work, in the summer of 1871, on a 'pastoral story', incorporating into it parts of this first, unpublished novel. He only mentions 'the accessories of one scene' as deriving from the earlier book, but there may well have been much more. When it was finished, he sent it to Macmillan, accompanied by the following letter:

7 August 1871

Gentlemen,

I have sent by railway the manuscript of a tale called 'Under the Greenwood Tree'.

It is entirely a story of rural life, and the attempt has been to draw the characters humorously, without caricature. General reasons have induced me to try my hand on a story wholly of this tone—one reason being some reviews of a late novel of mine—(in its leading features of a different nature from the present). In that story the rustic characters and scenery had very little point, yet to my surprise they were made very much of by the reviews. The *Athenaeum* said 'the characters are often exceedingly good ...

the parish clerk "a sort of Bowdlerized rake" who refers to the time "before he took orders" is really almost worthy of George Eliot . . . We see no reason why the author should not write novels but little, if at all inferior to the best of the present generation.' The *Spectator* said 'there is an *unusual* and *very* happy facility in catching and fixing phrases of peasant life—in producing for us, not the manners and language only but the tone of thought . . . and simple humour of consequential village worthies and gaping village rustics. So that we are irresistibly reminded of the paintings of Wilkie and still more perhaps of those of Teniers, etc. The scenes allotted to these humble actors are few and slight, but they indicate powers that might, and ought to be extended largely in this direction.' They then animadverted on the plot—though, such is the contradictoriness of reviews—this was the element which received the most unqualified praise in the *Morning Post*.

This however has nothing to do with the present tale. The accessories of one scene in it may possibly be recognised by you as appearing originally in a tale submitted a long time ago (which never saw the light). They were introduced advisedly, as giving a good background to the love portion.

I trust that your opinion of the work may be favourable, but in any case I shall be extremely glad to have your remarks on the manuscript.

Faithfully yours,
Thomas Hardy

This next letter is in reply to a request from Macmillan for the name of the published novel:

17 August 1871

Sir,

I have delayed my reply till I could send you perfect copies of the reviews which appeared—the extracts sent having been taken from notes I made in my pocket book at the time. The novel was *Desperate Remedies*, and the manuscript was submitted to you in the first place.

If you have time to read the reviews you will perceive that each takes for commendation a different element, and that they were therefore useless as guides to me for my second story. It seemed however that upon the whole a pastoral story would be the *safest* venture.

The article in the *Spectator* seemed strange enough to me—my object in the story having been simply to *construct* an intricate puzzle which nobody should guess till the end—and the characters were, to myself, mere puppets or pegs to weave the work upon—without reality or character enough in them to warrant their being denounced for want of moral attributes—the villain being in fact just about as human as the giants slain by Jack, and capable of corrupting to the same degree. This the *Spectator* did not see—or would not, and produced an article which contradicts itself, most noticeably. A novel which was good enough to justify two columns of lauded quotation could not possibly be so bad as to warrant opening remarks that are really little else than personalities. Still, being on the weaker side, I thought it just as well not to dabble in plot again at present, even though both *Athenaeum* and *Morning Post* thought the 'power' lay there.

Yours faithfully
Thomas Hardy

John Morley read the novel for Macmillan, and reported favourably as follows:

The work in this story is extremely careful, natural and delicate, and the writer deserves more than common credit for the pains which he has taken with his style and with the harmony of his construction and treatment. It is a simple and uneventful sketch of a rural courtship, with a moderate and reserved climax of real delicacy of idea. The writer is wanting in the fine poetic breath which gives such a charm to George Sand's work in the same kind, but he has evidently a true artistic feeling, if it is somewhat in excess of the feeling of a realist.

The opening scenes at the cottage on the Xmas Eve are quite twice as long as they ought to be, because the writer has not sufficient sparkle and humour to pass off such minute and prolonged description of a trifle.—*This part should decidedly be shortened.*

It would only, I suppose, make a one-volume story. I don't prophesy a large market for it, because the work is so delicate as not to hit every taste by any means. But it is good work, and would please people whose taste is not ruined by novels of exaggerated action or forced ingenuity. The writer would do well—

1. To study George Sand's best work.
2. To shut his ears to the fooleries of critics, as his letter to you proves he does not do.
3. To beware of letting *realism* grow out of proportion to his *fancy*.

After some hesitation and further correspondence, Macmillan

declined to publish the book immediately, and returned the MS. to Hardy. The *Early Life* reports Hardy's own story, that he had misinterpreted Macmillan's letter as a rejection, and had asked for the MS. back; but this is not true. The book was then offered to Tinsley Brothers, and published by them early in June 1872. The following year it was published in New York by Holt & Williams, the first of Hardy's novels to appear in America.

Pall Mall Gazette, 5 July 1872

This novel is as its second title informs us, a rural painting of the Dutch school, and a very carefully executed painting too. It portrays the vicissitudes of a village choir and the loves of a simple pair with so much freshness and originality that those happy persons who have leisure and opportunity to sit 'under the greenwood tree' could hardly do better than choose it for a companion. The only objection that might be made to the book is one greatly to the reader's advantage. The humble heroes and heroines of the tale are much too shrewd, and say too many good things, to be truthful representatives of their prototypes in real life. The conversations between the members of the choir are about the best things in the book. On one occasion they complain of the decay of the old-fashioned style of church music:—

> 'It served some of the village choirs right,' said one of the party. 'They should have stuck to strings as we did, and keep out clar'nets and done away with serpents. If you'd thrive in musical religion, stick to strings, says I.' 'There's worse things than serpents,' said Mr. Penny. 'Old things pass away, 'tis true; but a serpent was a good old note: a deep, rich note was the serpent.'

Clarionets are objected to as not made for the service of Providence; 'you can see it by looking at 'em.' . . .

. . . The rural party given by the tranter or carrier, at which Dick Dewy, the hero, and Miss Fancy Day, the heroine, meet, is well described—certainly no frequenter of parties, rural or otherwise, can deny the truth to nature of the host's observation, 'I assure you, neighbours,' he said, 'the heat of my frame no tongue can tell!' The village idiot appears in this picture of country life, but he is little less sharp than his companions. A deputation to the clergyman on musical business is proposed by the choir, but Thomas

Leaf is considered 'so terrible silly that he might ruin the concern,' and is to be left behind.

'I never had no head,' said Leaf, 'but I can sing my treble; and if Jim had lived I should have had a clever brother. To-morrow is poor Jim's birthday. He'd ha' been twenty-six if he'd lived till to-morrow.' 'You always seem very sorry for Jim,' said old William, musingly. 'Ah! I do. Such a stay to mother as he'd always ha' been! She'd never have had to work in her old age if he had continued strong—poor Jim!' 'What was his age when 'a died?' 'Four hours and twenty minutes—poor Jim! 'A was born as might be at night, and 'a didn't last as might be till the morning. No, 'a didn't last.' 'Well, Leaf, you shall come wi' us, as yours is such a melancholy family,' said old William, rather sadly.

The choir has occupied us more than the love story. Although prettily told, it is considerably marred by an episode regarding the vicar which destroys the simple character of the tale, otherwise well maintained throughout.

The Saturday Review, 28 September 1872

This novel is the best prose idyl that we have seen for a long while past. Deserting the more conventional, and far less agreeable, field of imaginative creation, which he worked in his earlier book, called *Desperate Remedies,* the author has produced a series of rural pictures full of life and genuine colouring, and drawn with a distinct minuteness reminding one at times of some of the scenes in *Hermann und Dorothea.* Any one who knows tolerably well the remoter parts of the South-Western counties of England will be able to judge for himself of the power and truthfulness shown in these studies of the better class of rustics, men whose isolated lives have not impaired a shrewd common sense and insight, together with a complete independence, set off by native humour, which is excellently represented in these two volumes.

Reuben Dewy, the 'tranter' or irregular carrier, is the principal character in the book, and is the most fully worked-out type of the class we have been mentioning. At the very outset of events, during the rounds made by the Christmas 'waits' of Mellstock parish church, Dick Dewy, the son and partner of Reuben, falls in love with Fancy Day, daughter of a neighbouring keeper well to do in the world, and newly appointed schoolmistress of the parish. The 'course of true love' in this simple village couple, interrupted only by the gawky attentions of Mr. Shinar, a wealthy farmer and churchwarden, and by a curious episode with the vicar towards the end, forms the unpretending thread of the story. But the subsidiary scenes, such as the description of the carol-singers' rounds, the village-party at the tranter's, the interview of the choir with the vicar, and the bee-taking at the keeper Geoffrey Day's, are worked in with as much care as if the writer had been constructing a sensation plot of the received model; and each one of these scenes contributes its share to a really pleasant and entertaining whole.

Under the Greenwood Tree is filled with touches showing the close sympathy with which the writer has watched the life, not only of his fellow-men in the country hamlets, but of woods and fields and all the outward forms of nature. But the staple of the book is made up of personal sketches, the foremost figure, as we have said, being that of the 'tranter' Dewy, a man 'full of human nature,' fond of broaching his cider with his village friends about him, straightforward and outspoken, yet inclined from good nature towards compromise, not however to the excessive degree that his duties as publican imposed upon Mr. Snell in *Silas Marner*. Grouped around the tranter are several figures, all distinctive and good in their way, the chief of whom are old William Dewy, the grandfather, and the leader in all things musical, Mr. Penny the bootmaker, and Thomas Leaf, who sang treble in the choir at a preternaturally late date, and whose upper G could not be dispensed with, though he was otherwise 'deficient,' and awkward in his movements, 'apparently on account of having grown so fast that before he had had time to grow used to his height he was higher.' The description of the old choir-leader is too good to be passed over:—

His was a humorous and gentle nature, not unmixed with a frequent melancholy; and he had a firm religious faith. But to his neighbours he had no character in particular. If they saw him pass by their windows when they had been bottling off old mead, or when they had just been called long-headed men who might do anything in the world if they chose, they thought concerning him, 'Ah, there's that good-hearted man—open as a child!' If they saw him just after losing a shilling or half-a-crown, or accidentally letting fall a piece of crockery, they thought, 'There's that poor weak-minded man Dewy again! Ah, he'll never do much in the world either!' If he passed when fortune neither smiled nor frowned on them, they merely thought him old William Dewy.

We doubt whether the night's doings of a party of carol-singers have ever been half so well told as in this novel.

The whole interview with the parson is excellent reading, and deserves more notice than we can bestow on it here. It is strong praise of any book to say that, besides being a novel of great humour and general merit, it would make no bad manual for any one who, from duty or from choice, is desirous to learn something of the inner life of a rural parish. Yet *Under the Greenwood Tree* fairly deserves that amount of praise. It is a book that might well lie on the table of any well-ordered country house, and that might also be borne in mind by the readers during kindly rounds undertaken among the cottages. There are, to be sure, weak points in the writing. The love passages of Dick and Fancy incline here and there to be unnecessarily prolonged, and it is needful throughout to recollect that they are being faithfully drawn as *rustic* lovers. There is also one definite fault in the dialogues, though it makes its appearance only at wide intervals. We mean an occasional tendency of the country folk, not so much to think with something of subtle distinction (for cottagers can do that much more completely than the well-dressed world are apt to suppose), but to express themselves in the language of the author's manner of thought, rather than in their own. The tranter, for example, should not be allowed to call the widow Leaf (in an otherwise very amusing passage) an 'imaginative woman on the subject of children'; nor should old William speak of barrel-organs and harmoniums, even though he has wound himself up for a great effort, as 'miserable machines for such a divine thing as music.' . . .

. . . Regarded as a whole, we repeat our opinion that the book is one of unusual merit in its own special line, full of humour and keen observation, and with the genuine air of the country breathing throughout it.   [HORACE MOULE]

¶ Both these reviews were kept by Hardy, and pasted in his scrapbook. Both quote freely, and retell several of the episodes in the book, and we have therefore abridged them: but retaining almost all their comments. *The Saturday Review*'s notice was by Horace Moule, Hardy's friend and patron: even more than the *Pall Mall* critic, Moule obviously enjoyed the book, and can hardly stop quoting and describing. The one piece of plot machinery in the novel is mentioned only briefly and uncertainly by both critics:

the *Pall Mall* thought it 'considerably marred' the love story, but *The Saturday Review*, in a paragraph not included above, said,

> 'Serious mischief threatens for a moment, just towards the close, on the side of the Vicar; but this episode, whether wisely introduced or not, is too brief to signify much in the working out of the story.'

Both critics fastened on what was to become a common criticism of Hardy's later novels, the tendency of the rustics (here *The Saturday Review* has the severer wording) 'to express themselves in the language of the author's manner of thought, rather than in their own'. And of course they both linger on what was and is Hardy's greatest praise, his creation of the rural community. 'The genuine air of the country breathes through it.'

3 · FAR FROM THE MADDING CROWD

❰ *Far from the Madding Crowd* was written during 1873 and the first half of 1874. In September 1873, Hardy sent some of it to Leslie Stephen, editor of the *Cornhill*, who accepted it at once, though it was not yet finished. It appeared as a serial in the *Cornhill* throughout 1874, and was published as a book by Smith, Elder and Co. on 23 November 1874, and a few days earlier by Henry Holt in America.

The Spectator, 3 January 1874

The readers of the *Cornhill* are to be congratulated doubly this time,—on the conclusion of 'Zelda's Fortune,' and on the commencement of an anonymous novel so clever and so remarkable, that though speculation upon the authorship may be indiscreet, it is irresistible. If 'Far from the Madding Crowd' is not written by George Eliot, then there is a new light among novelists. In every page of these introductory chapters there are a dozen sentences which have the ring of the wit and the wisdom of the only truly great English novelist now living. The description of Gabriel Oak is too perfect, for it will not bear curtailment, but it has such extractible characteristics as these:—'He was at the brightest period of masculine life, for his intellect and his emotions were clearly separated; he had passed the time during which the influence of youth indiscriminately mingles them in the character of impulse, and he had not yet arrived at the stage wherein they become united again, in the character of prejudice, by the influence of a wife and family. In short, he was twenty-eight, and a bachelor. . . . Fitness being the basis of all beauty, nobody could have denied that his steady swings and turns in and about the flock had elements of grace. Yet, although if occasion demanded he could do or think a thing with as mercurial a dash as can the men of towns, who are more to the manner born, his special power, morally, physically, and mentally, was static, owing little or nothing to momentum as a rule.' Then the beautiful girl with whom Farmer Oak falls in love is described in passages which bear internal evidence; here is one:—'There was a bright air and manner about her now, by which she seemed to imply that the desirability of her existence could not be questioned, and this rather saucy assumption failed in being offensive, because a beholder felt it to be, on the whole, true. Like exceptional emphasis in the tone of a genius, that which would have made mediocrity ridiculous was an addition to recognised power.' And the inarticulateness of Gabriel:—'He wished she knew his impressions; but he would as soon have thought of carrying an odour in a net, as of attempting to convey the intangibilities of his feeling in the coarse meshes of language.' There is a passage descriptive of the companionship of the stars, so learned and so poetical that it seems to be irrefutable evidence of the authorship. At all events, the *Cornhill* is giving us a high intellectual treat this time, and we are not the less grateful because it is certainly due as reparation. [R. H. HUTTON]

Letter from Leslie Stephen, 12 March 1874

... I have ventured to leave out a line or two in the last batch of proofs from an excessive prudery of which I am ashamed; but one is forced to be absurdly particular. May I suggest that Troy's seduction of the young woman will require to be treated in a gingerly fashion when, as I suppose must be the case, he comes to be exposed to his wife? I mean that the thing must be stated but that the words must be careful—excuse this wretched shred of concession to popular stupidity; but I am a slave ...

Letter from Leslie Stephen, 13 April 1874

... The cause of Fanny's death is unnecessarily emphasized ... I have some doubts whether the baby is necessary at all ... It certainly rather injures the story, and perhaps if the omission were made it might be restored on republication. ...

The Examiner, 5 December 1874

... When the first chapters of 'Far from the Madding Crowd' appeared in the *Cornhill Magazine*, a supposition was started that this must be a new novel by George Eliot, and the point was very generally discussed. Indeed, if those chapters stood by themselves as a fragment of unknown authorship, no conjecture could be more plausible: they deal with the kind of life that George Eliot has more than once chosen to describe, to which, in fact, she has almost acquired a prescriptive right, and the opening description of Farmer Oak is a portrait very much in her manner. If the critic cared to go into minute corroborations of such distinguished parentage, he would find them in the incidents of Bathsheba's unpacking the mirror and taking a survey of her beauty while waiting on the top of the cart, and her higgling over twopence with the toll-keeper: these little incidents have a delicate spice of malicious truth to nature which one often finds in George Eliot's pictures. At the same time, if we had read Mr. Hardy's previous novels, we need have had no difficulty in tracing the authorship of 'Far From the Madding Crowd,' for Mr. Hardy's style is his own and sufficiently distinctive to be easily recognised. One might mistake a detached portion of his work for George Eliot's, but when it is viewed as a whole it has a good many striking points of difference. Mr. Hardy is not such a master of language as George Eliot: his style has not the same freshness, nor the same eloquence and momentum. And this difference of style goes along with a more deeply-seated difference of matter: Mr. Hardy is much less of a preacher than George Eliot; his interests are more exclusively dramatic, he is absorbed in delineating character and tracing the workings of passion by minute touches, and does not withdraw from his dramatic work to deliver his soul of pent-up reflections. With all George Eliot's impartiality towards her creations, and her desire to represent each one's life truly as it is, nothing extenuating nor setting down aught in malice, the heart of the preacher is to be detected in her choice of subjects: her characters derive a large part of their interest from their opinions and views of life. Now the drama in Mr. Hardy's novels is no sense a warfare of opinions or ideas: it is a warfare of persons, persons moved by the primeval motives of love and jealousy. 'Far From the Madding Crowd' is concerned with no deeper mysteries than women's hearts, and how they are lost and won: its story lies in country fields and farm-houses, and occupies itself solely with the secular and social life of the inhabitants. Whether we regard this as a merit or a defect or a matter of indifference depends entirely on our conceptions of art and its functions: but if we hold no dogma concerning the functions of art, and approach Mr. Hardy's novel simply as a drama, willing to believe that it need not be frivolous because it has no great lesson to teach, it is impossible not to recognise the novelist's power . . .

The Spectator, 19 December 1874

No one who reads this very original and amusing story will doubt for a moment that it is the production of a very high order of ability and humour. Everything in the book is fresh, and almost everything in the book is striking. The life of the agricultural districts in the South-Western counties—Dorsetshire probably—is a new field for the novelist, and at least so far as the physical forms of nature and the external features of the farm-work are concerned, it has been mastered by the author of this tale. The details of the farming and the sheep-keeping, of the labouring, the feasting, and the mourning, are painted with all the vividness of a powerful imagination, painting from the stores of a sharply-outlined memory. The reader sees in turn the life of the shepherd in lambing-time, of the bailiff and his out-door labourers at the homestead, of the mistress on her pay-day, the interior of the malt-house and its gossip, the corn-market at the county town, the thunder-storm which breaks up the fine harvest weather, the rural inn and its company, the sheep-fair on the downs, the tenant-farmer's Christmas merry-making or effort at merry-making, and the village group which watches the entrance of the Judge into the Assize town; and from everything he reads he carries away new images, and as it were, new experience, taken from the life of a region before almost unknown. A book like this is, in relation to many of the scenes it describes, the nearest equivalent to actual experience which a great many of us are ever likely to boast of. But the very certainty we feel that this is the case—that we have no adequate means of checking a good deal of the very fresh and evidently closely-observed detail which we find in this book—puts us upon asking all the more anxiously whether all the vivacious description we have here is quite trustworthy, not only in its picture of the scenery and ways of life, but in its picture of the human beings who give the chief interest to that scenery and those ways of life. And here the reader who has any general acquaintance with the civilisation of the Wiltshire or Dorsetshire labourer, with his average wages, and his average intelligence, will be disposed to say at once that a more incredible picture than that of the group of farm labourers as a whole which Mr. Hardy has given us can hardly be conceived,—that he has filled his canvas with an assemblage of all the exceptional figures which a quick-witted humorist might discover here and there and sift with much pains out of a whole county; that if any one society of agricultural labourers were at all like that which we find here, that class, as a whole, must be a treasure-house of such eccentric shrewdness and profane-minded familiarity with the Bible, as would cancel at once the reputation rural England has got for a heavy, bovine character, and would justify us in believing it to be a rich mine of quaintnesses and oddities, all dashed with a curious flavour of mystical and Biblical transcendentalism. Even in the delineations of the less humble characters there is plenty of reason to suspect that Mr. Hardy has from time to time embodied in the objects of his studies some of the subtler thoughts which they have suggested to his own mind, or some of the more cultivated metaphors to which he would himself have given utterance had he been in their place, but which come most unnaturally from the mouths from which they actually proceed. Thus when the farm-labourers are coming up to be paid, the maltster's great grand-daughter, Liddy Smallbury, who is the farming heroine's humble companion,—half-friend, half-servant,—announces this event to her mistress in the words, 'The Philistines are upon us!' just as an art critic might say when the general public swarm in on the day of a private view; and again, the old maltster, who can't either count or speak English, is made to say, when moralising on the uprooting of an apple-tree and the transformation of a pump, with an extravagance that must be intended for broad humour, 'How the face of nations alter, and what great revolutions we live to see now-a-days!' Nay, even the poorest creatures in the story break out into the same kind of intellectual banter, not only at times, but almost habitually. For instance, Jan Coggan, a rural labourer, who, on his first introduction, is delineated as the joker of his class, though an elderly member of it, is described as bantering a poor fellow named Laban Tall (who is under the strict dominion of a wife he has just married), on his early retreat from their social gathering, in the following words, 'New lords, new laws, as the saying is!'—a remark, as it seems to us, of quite another moral latitude and longitude, just as the repeater-watch which, it appears, on the occasion of a drunken revel in the barn—in celebration of the harvest and of the mistress's marriage—that the same Jan Coggan carries in his waistcoat-pocket, seems to suggest a totally different world of physical belongings. But the peculiarity, as we have already hinted, of this tale is, that not merely one or two, but almost all the labourers introduced in it talk in a peculiar style, deeply infiltrated with the suggestions of a kind of moral irony mostly borrowed, no doubt, from the study of the Bible, but still applied in a manner in which neither uneducated Churchmen nor uneducated Dissenters—(and these people are all of the Church)—would dream of applying it. When Mause

Headrigg, in *Old Mortality*, says, 'By the aid of my God I have leaped over a wall,' the humour is in the novelist, not in her who applies the text in grim puritanic seriousness. But when Bathsheba Everdene reproaches her servant, Maryann Money, 'a person who for a face had a circular disc, furrowed less by age than by long gazes of perplexity at distant objects,' with not being married and off her hands, and that individual replies, 'What between the poor men I won't have, and the rich men who won't have me, I stand forlorn as a pelican in the wilderness,—ah poor soul of me!' we recognise at once the introduction of a satiric vein belonging to the author's own mental plane into the language of a class very far removed from it. The same traces of an intellectual graft on coarse and vulgar thoughts are visible in every one of the many amusing and often most humorous conversations recorded in this book. The whole class of hoers, sowers, ploughmen, reapers, &c., are—if Mr. Hardy's pictures may be trusted—the most incredibly amusing and humorous persons you ever came across,—full of the quaintest irony and the most comical speculative intelligence. Mrs. Gamp is an impossible though most amusing impersonation of the monthly nurse. But Mrs. Gamp makes no claim to any shrewdness beyond the shrewdness of the most profound selfishness; for the rest, she is only a delightful and impossible concentration of the essence of all conceivable monthly-nurse experiences. But these poor men are quizzical critics, inaccurate divines, keen-eyed men of the world, who talk a semi-profane, semi-Biblical dialect full of veins of humour which have passed into it from a different sphere.

Mr. Hardy himself has adopted a style of remark on his own imaginative creations which is an exaggeration of George Eliot's, but he has made the mistake which George Eliot never makes, of blending a good deal of this same style of thought with the substance of his drawings. . . .   [R. H. HUTTON]

The Nation (New York), 24 December 1874

Mr. Hardy's novel came into the world under brilliant auspices— such as the declaration by the London *Spectator* that either George Eliot had written it or George Eliot had found her match. One could make out in a manner what the *Spectator* meant. To guess, one has only to open 'Far from the Madding Crowd' at random: 'Mr. Jan Coggan, who had passed the cup to Henery, was a crimson man with a spacious countenance and a private glimmer in his eye, whose name had appeared on the marriage register of Weatherbury

and neighboring parishes as best-man and chief witness in countless unions of the previous twenty years; he also very frequently
filled the post of head godfather in baptisms of the subtly-jovial
kind.' That is a very fair imitation of George Eliot's humorous
manner. Here is a specimen of her serious one: 'He fancied he had
felt himself in the penumbra of a very deep sadness when touching
that slight and fragile creature. But wisdom lies in moderating
mere impressions, and Gabriel endeavored to think little of this.'
But the *Spectator's* theory had an even broader base, and we may
profitably quote a passage which perhaps constituted one of its
solidest blocks. The author of 'Silas Marner' has won no small part
of her fame by her remarkable faculty as a reporter of ale-house
and kitchen-fire conversations among simple-minded rustics. Mr.
Hardy has also made a great effort in this direction, and here is a
specimen—a particularly favorable specimen—of his success:

'"Why, Joseph Poorgrass, you han't had a drop!" said Mr.
Coggan to a very shrinking man in the background, thrusting
the cup towards him.

'"Such a shy man as he is," said Jacob Smallbury, "Why,
ye've hardly had strength of eye enough to look in our young
mis'ess's face, so I hear, Joseph?"

'All looked at Joseph Poorgrass with pitying reproach.

'"No, I've hardly looked at her at all," faltered Joseph,
reducing his body smaller while talking, apparently from a meek
sense of undue prominence; "and when I see'd her, it was nothing
but blushes with me!"

'"Poor fellow," said Mr. Clark.

'" 'Tis a curious nature for a man," said Jan Coggan.

'"Yes," continued Joseph Poorgrass, his shyness, which was
so painful as a defect, just beginning to fill him with a little com-
placency, now that it was regarded in the light of an interesting
study. " 'Twere blush, blush, blush with me every minute of the
time when she was speaking to me."

'"I believe ye, Joseph Poorgrass, for we all know ye to be a
very bashful man."

'" 'Tis terrible bad for a man, poor soul!" said the maltster.
"And how long have ye suffered from it, Joseph?"

'"Oh, ever since I was a boy. Yes—mother was concerned to
her heart about it—yes. But 'twas all naught."

'"Did ye ever take anything to try and stop it, Joseph Poorgrass?"

'"Oh, aye, tried all sorts. They took me to Greenhill Fair, and into a great large jerry-go-nimble show, where there were women-folk riding round—standing up on horses, with hardly anything on but their smocks; but it didn't cure me a morsel—no, not a morsel. And then I was put errand-man at the Woman's Skittle Alley at the back of the Tailor's Arms in Casterbridge. 'Twas a horrible gross situation, and altogether a very curious place for a good man. I had to stand and look at wicked people in the face from morning till night; but 'twas no use—I was just as bad as ever after all. Blushes have been in the family for generations. There, 'tis a happy providence I be no worse, so to speak it—yes, a happy thing, and I feel my few poor gratitudes."'

This is extremely clever, and the author has evidently read to good purpose the low-life chapters in George Eliot's novels; he has caught very happily her trick of seeming to humor benignantly her queer people and look down at them from the heights of ana-lytic omniscience. But we have quoted the episode because it seems to us an excellent example of the cleverness which is only clever-ness, of the difference between original and imitative talent—the disparity, which it is almost unpardonable not to perceive, between first-rate talent and those inferior grades which range from second-rate downward, and as to which confusion is a more venial offence. Mr. Hardy puts his figures through a variety of comical movements; he fills their mouths with quaint turns of speech; he baptizes them with odd names ('Joseph Poorgrass' for a bashful, easily-snubbed Dissenter is excellent); he pulls the wires, in short, and produces a vast deal of sound and commotion; and his novel, at a cursory glance, has a rather promising air of life and warmth. But by critics who prefer a grain of substance to a pound of shadow it will, we think, be pronounced a decidedly delusive performance; it has a fatal lack of magic. We have found it hard to read, but its short-comings are easier to summarize than to encounter in order. Mr. Hardy's novel is very long, but his subject is very short and simple, and the work has been distended to its rather formidable dimen-sions by the infusion of a large amount of conversational and descriptive padding and the use of an ingeniously verbose and redundant style. It is inordinately diffuse, and, as a piece of narra-tive, singularly inartistic. The author has little sense of proportion, and almost none of composition. We learn about Bathsheba and Gabriel, Farmer Boldwood and Sergeant Troy, what we can rather than what we should; for Mr. Hardy's inexhaustible faculty for spinning smart dialogue makes him forget that dialogue in a story is after all but episode, and that a novelist is after all but a historian, thoroughly possessed of certain facts, and bound in some way or other to impart them. To tell a story almost exclusively by reporting people's talks is the most difficult art in the world, and really leads, logically, to a severe economy in the use of rejoinder and repartee, and not to a lavish expenditure of them. 'Far from the Madding Crowd' gives us an uncomfortable sense of being a simple 'tale,' pulled and stretched to make the conventional three volumes; and the author, in his long-sustained appeal to one's attention, reminds us of a person fishing with an enormous net, of which the meshes should be thrice too wide.

We are happily not subject, in this (as to minor matters) much-emancipated land, to the tyranny of the three volumes; but we confess that we are nevertheless being rapidly urged to a conviction that (since it is in the nature of fashions to revolve and recur) the day has come round again for some of the antique restrictions as to literary form. The three unities, in Aristotle's day, were inexorably imposed on Greek tragedy: why shouldn't we have something of the same sort for English fiction in the day of Mr. Hardy? Almost all novels are greatly too long, and the being too long becomes with each elapsing year a more serious offence. Mr. Hardy begins with a detailed description of his hero's smile, and proceeds thence to give a voluminous account of his large silver watch. Gabriel Oak's smile and his watch were doubtless respectable and important phenomena; but everything is relative, and daily becoming more so; and we confess that, as a hint of the pace at which the author proposed to proceed, his treatment of these facts produced upon us a deterring and depressing effect. If novels were the only books written, novels written on this scale would be all very well; but as they compete, in the esteem of sensible people, with a great many other books, and a great many other objects of interest of all kinds, we are inclined to think that, in the long run, they will be defeated in the struggle for existence unless they lighten their baggage very considerably and do battle in a more scientific equipment. Therefore, we really imagine that a few arbitrary rules —a kind of depleting process—might have a wholesome effect. It might be enjoined, for instance, that no 'tale' should exceed fifty pages and no novel two hundred; that a plot should have but such and such a number of ramifications; that no ramification should have more than a certain number of persons; that no person should utter more than a given number of words; and that no description of an inanimate object should consist of more than a fixed number of lines. We should not incline to advocate this oppressive legislation as a comfortable or ideal finality for the romancer's art, but

we think it might be excellent as a transitory discipline or drill.
Necessity is the mother of invention, and writers with a powerful
tendency to expatiation might in this temporary strait-jacket be
induced to transfer their attention rather more severely from quantity to quality. The use of the strait-jacket would have cut down
Mr. Hardy's novel to half its actual length and, as he is a clever
man, have made the abbreviated work very ingeniously pregnant.
We should have had a more occasional taste of all the barn-yard
worthies—Joseph Poorgrass, Laban Tall, Matthew Moon, and the
rest—and the vagaries of Miss Bathsheba would have had a more
sensible consistency. Our restrictions would have been generous,
however, and we should not have proscribed such a fine passage as
this:

'Then there came a third flash. Manœuvres of the most extraordinary kind were going on in the vast firmamental hollows
overhead. The lightning now was the color of silver, and gleamed
in the heavens like a mailed army. Rumbles became rattles.
Gabriel, from his elevated position, could see over the landscape
for at least half a dozen miles in front. Every hedge, bush, and
tree was distinct as in a line engraving. In a paddock in the same
direction was a herd of heifers, and the forms of these were visible
at this moment in the act of galloping about in the wildest and
maddest confusion, flinging their heels and tails high into the air,
their heads to earth. A poplar in the immediate foreground was
like an ink-stroke on burnished tin. Then the picture vanished,
leaving a darkness so intense that Gabriel worked entirely by
feeling with his hands.'

Mr. Hardy describes nature with a great deal of felicity, and is
evidently very much at home among rural phenomena. The most
genuine thing in his book, to our sense, is a certain aroma of the
meadows and lanes—a natural relish for harvesting and sheep-
washings. He has laid his scene in an agricultural county, and his
characters are children of the soil—unsophisticated country-folk.
Bathsheba Everdene is a rural heiress, left alone in the world, in
possession of a substantial farm. Gabriel Oak is her shepherd,
Farmer Boldwood is her neighbor, and Sergeant Troy is a loose
young soldier who comes a-courting her. They are all in love with
her, and the young lady is a flirt, and encourages them all. Finally
she marries the Sergeant, who has just seduced her maid-servant.
The maid-servant dies in the work-house, the Sergeant repents,
leaves his wife, and is given up for drowned. But he reappears and
is shot by Farmer Boldwood, who delivers himself up to justice.

Bathsheba then marries Gabriel Oak, who has loved and waited in silence, and is, in our opinion, much too good for her. The chief purpose of the book is, we suppose, to represent Gabriel's dumb, devoted passion, his biding his time, his rendering unsuspected services to the woman who has scorned him, his integrity and simplicity and sturdy patience. In all this the tale is very fairly successful, and Gabriel has a certain vividness of expression. But we cannot say that we either understand or like Bathsheba. She is a young lady of the inconsequential, wilful, mettlesome type which has lately become so much the fashion for heroines, and of which Mr. Charles Reade is in a manner the inventor—the type which aims at giving one a very intimate sense of a young lady's *womanishness*. But Mr. Hardy's embodiment of it seems to us to lack reality; he puts her through the Charles Reade paces, but she remains alternately vague and coarse, and seems always artificial. This is Mr. Hardy's trouble; he rarely gets beyond ambitious artifice—the mechanical simulation of heat and depth and wisdom that are absent. Farmer Boldwood is a shadow, and Sergeant Troy an elaborate stage-figure. Everything human in the book strikes us as factitious and insubstantial; the only things we believe in are the sheep and the dogs. But, as we say, Mr. Hardy has gone astray very cleverly, and his superficial novel is a really curious imitation of something better.   HENRY JAMES

The Observer, 3 January 1875

This is a wonderfully clever book, with all its absurdities, improprieties (we do not mean moral improprieties), incongruities, and suddenly sensational incidents; but we cannot for our lives understand how any person of ordinary penetration, much more a skilled critic, could ever have supposed it to be written by George Eliot. The author of *Romola* and *The Mill on the Floss* is a great artist, too much of an artist sometimes. The author of *Far from the Madding Crowd* is a dauber by comparison; but if a dauber at all, a dauber who throws on the colours, and arranges the figures, and manages the composition with a vast deal of reckless skill. His ingenuity is greater than George Eliot's; but whilst she knows more of human nature than all of us put together, he knows just about as much of it as the simplest of us, and no more. His observations are admirably set forth sometimes, and are always appropriate; but they are only our own observations put epigrammatically—not new ones, by any means, as George Eliot's are. In one respect, as concerns that great writer, we are inclined to thank him warmly. He has shown how easily an exceedingly bad habit—indeed, trick—into which she has of late, and more especially in *Middlemarch*, permitted herself to fall, can be imitated; and we sincerely hope she will read this book in order to be cured of a bit of unfortunate originality that can be copied with such facility. It is she herself who says that one never quite knows the value of one's own opinions till they come back to one exaggerated and travestied by other people. It would perhaps be difficult to exaggerate or to travesty some of the solemn amplifications and involutions of very simple truths which are to be met with in *Middlemarch*. But here, at least, is a good specimen in the way of imitation:—'On Sundays he was a man of misty views, rather given to a postponing treatment of things, whose best clothes and seven-and-sixpenny umbrella were always hampering him; upon the whole, one who felt himself to occupy morally that vast middle space of Laodicean neutrality which lay between the Sacrament people of the parish and the drunken division of its inhabitants.'... We would cite a good many instances of the same character: but it would be superfluous to do so, as our object is simply to warn Mr. Hardy against a rock that he seems fond of bumping against, and if it be not presumptuous to say so, to show a still cleverer writer even than Mr. Hardy how easily her semi-scientific reflections about nothing can be copied. We are perfectly aware that there are people who admire this 'Mesopotamian' sort of thing; and doubtless the sentences we have cited were precisely those which led them to imagine that this book was by George Eliot. Indeed, so great is their admiration for it, that they confound it with the real 'wit and wisdom' by that immortal authoress. In our opinion these solemn mystifications of the simple are neither wit nor wisdom.

Having relieved our consciences of this burden, we will again say that *Far from the Madding Crowd* is a wonderfully clever book, and, we will add, an uncommonly interesting one. Like all good stories, it lets one down at the last, and the end of the second volume is disappointing. We are not satisfied by the death of Sergeant Troy, who, if punished at all, should have been punished very differently, nor with Farmer Boldwood's insanity, nor even with poor Gabriel Oak's marriage. We should not like to be confounded with those critics who insist that a book ought to end 'satisfactorily' for the sake of the reader's feelings. There are two kinds of novels; the first or highest sort, in which the novel ends itself, so to speak, and decrees its own termination, as action in real life does, and in such cases we do not inquire whether our feelings are soothed or lacerated, but only if the story and its *dénoument* be *true*. The

second kind of novel is that in which the characters and the march
of events are more or less puppets, which remain to the last under
the control of the narrator, who pulls the wires as he chooses. *Far
from the Madding Crowd* belongs to this second class; and since Mr.
Hardy displays a fine imaginative disregard for probability we have
a right to complain that he did not employ his absolute authority
in this story with more regard to the susceptibilities of human
nature. We confess we think it rather hard that a merely wilful
young woman with a pretty face should be wooed by three different
men, two of whom marry her, one of whom is killed for her, and the
third of whom she drives crazy. We are quite willing to acknowledge
that the power of her sex is considerable, but we think that a man
like Gabriel Oak would never have consented to accept Sergeant
Troy's and Farmer Boldwood's leavings. Perhaps, however, we are
troubling ourselves to criticise where criticism is superfluous, and
that Mr. Hardy would reply, 'Have I amused you? If I have that
is all I wanted.' We should be obliged to answer his question in the
affirmative. He is never dull, and rarely tiresome. But if such really
were his rejoinder we should be disposed to say that he rated his
powers much too cheaply. We are convinced he could write a much
better book than *Far from the Madding Crowd*, which would be
equally entertaining. His keen love and penetrating eye for the
face, changes and operations of Nature, his sly humour, his conversational power—though this is a little forced sometimes, and his
talent for describing things briskly and tersely, are great qualities
in a novelist. His one great want, it seems to us, is want of depth,
more especially in pourtraying character. No doubt, if he had dug
deeper into his characters in this story, the reader would have seen,
and he would himself have seen, the fundamental absurdity and
impossibility of much of the story. Even as it is, we never can
make up our minds whether Bathsheba Everdene is intended to be
a 'lady,' or the opposite; and it is quite certain that, on either
supposition, she could not have done what she is represented as
doing. The truth is, she is sometimes presented to the reader in one
aspect, and sometimes in the other, just as it suits the author's
convenience. Gabriel Oak is outlined with much the same sort of
ambiguity, and so, to a great extent are Sergeant Troy and Farmer
Boldwood. The first interview between Troy and Bathsheba represents the latter in so odious a light, if women in whatever rank of
society, are supposed to retain any trace of modesty and reserve,
that we confess we do not care one straw about her afterwards, and
are only sorry that Gabriel Oak was not sufficiently manly to refuse
to have anything more to say to such an incorrigible hussy.

Our readers will, therefore, perceive plainly that we think rather badly of Mr. Hardy's plot on the whole, and not very much of his characters. Nevertheless, we repeat it unhesitatingly, the novel in question is a very remarkable book. The descriptions of farming operations—lambing, sheep-shearing, and the rest—are admirably done, and, far from being gratuitously obtruded, are introduced most naturally and felicitously, and subserve the purposes of the narrator in a striking manner. . . .

The book is full of good things; and now and then we come across a bit of George Eliotism, which has the true ring—*e.g.* the following:—'We learn that it is not the rays which bodies absorb, but those which they reflect, that give them colours they are known by, and in the same way people are specialised by their dislikes and antagonisms, whilst their goodwill is looked upon as no attribute at all.' Still we should strongly advise Mr. Hardy to avoid this method of reflection even when the reflection seems true and apposite. We had marked several passages for quotation; but, on second thoughts, we will leave them where they stand, recommending everybody who cares for a novel to read this one. When they have done so, we think they will agree with us, that it is a strange jumble of great merit and grotesque faults, an interesting tale ending stupidly, and a panorama of impossible people under impossible circumstances, who contrive, nevertheless, to keep up our interest till the curtain falls.

The Saturday Review, 9 January 1875

Mr. Hardy still lingers in the pleasant byways of pastoral and agricultural life which he made familiar to his readers in his former novels, *Under the Greenwood Tree* and *A Pair of Blue Eyes*. Indeed the first of these can hardly be called a novel. It was rather a series of rustic sketches—Dutch paintings of English country scenes after the manner of *Silas Marner*. But, like its successor, *A Pair of Blue Eyes*, it brought with it a genuine fresh flavour of the country, and of a part of the country that has not yet become hackneyed. There was promise, too, in both these books of something really good being produced in future works. And that promise, though not quite fulfilled, is given again in *Far from the Madding Crowd*. It is nearer fulfilment than it was, though much nearer in the first half of the first volume than in the remainder of the book, where the characters both of the heroine and of the hero fall off. But there is still a good deal wanting, and Mr. Hardy has much to learn, or perhaps we ought to say, to unlearn, before he can be placed in the first order of modern English novelists. He takes trouble, and is not in a hurry to work off his sketches. They are imaginative, drawn from the inside, and highly finished. They show power also of probing and analysing the deeper shades of character, and showing how characters are affected, and how destinies are influenced for good or evil, by the circumstances which act upon them. But Mr. Hardy disfigures his pages by bad writing, by clumsy and inelegant metaphors, and by mannerism and affectation. What, for instance, could be worse as a piece of composition than the following?—

'His tone was so utterly removed from all she had expected as a beginning. It was lowness and quiet accented: an emphasis of deep meanings, their form, at the same time, being scarcely expressed. Silence has sometimes a remarkable power of showing itself as the disembodied soul of feeling wandering without its carcase, and it is then more impressive than speech.'

The grammar in this passage is faulty, and metaphor is far-fetched and awkward, the thought poor, and the expression of it affected. Again, how could a man of good taste—and good taste Mr. Hardy certainly has—permit this hideous metaphor to appear?—'It' ('the element of folly') 'was introduced as lymph on the dart of Eros, and eventually permeated and coloured her whole constitution.' A quack doctor before the days of Public Vaccinators might have written such a sentence as a taking advertisement. But a man of refinement, and not without a sense of humour, might surely have put the not unprecedented fact that a girl fell in love with a soldier in simpler and less professional language. Why, again, should he talk of Bathsheba's beauty 'belonging rather to the redeemed-demonian than to the blemished-angelic school,' or of 'a little slip of humanity for alarming potentialities of exploit,' or of 'the spherical completeness of his existence heretofore slowly spreading into an abnormal distortion in the particular direction of an ideal passion'? Eccentricities of style are not characteristic of genius, nor of original thinking. If Mr. Hardy is not possessed of genius, he is possessed of something quite good enough for the ordinary purposes of novel-writing to make him independent of anything like counterfeit originality or far-fetched modes of thought. If he has the self-control to throw aside his tendency to strain after metaphorical effects, and if he will cultivate simplicity of diction as effectually as he selects simple and natural subjects to write about, he may mellow into a considerable novelist. But if he suffers this tendency to grow into a habit—and there is quite as much of it in this as in his previous novels—he will very speedily lose the not inconsiderable reputation which he has justly gained.

Mr. Hardy, whether by force of circumstances or by fortunate selection, has in this story hit upon a new vein of rich metal for his fictitious scenes. The English Bœotian has never been so idealized before. Ordinary men's notions of the farm-labourer of the Southern counties have all been blurred and confused. It has been the habit of an ignorant and unwisely philanthropic age to look upon him as an untaught, unreflecting, badly paid, and badly fed animal, ground down by hard and avaricious farmers, and very little, if at all, raised by intelligence above the brutes and beasts to whom he ministers. These notions are ruthlessly overturned by Mr. Hardy's novel. Under his hand Bœotians become Athenians in acuteness, Germans in capacity for philosophic speculation, and Parisians in polish. Walter Scott has left many sketches and some highly finished portraits of the humbler class of Scotch peasants, and has brought out the national shrewdness and humour, and the moral and intellectual 'pawkiness' for which that class of Scotch society is justly celebrated. But he had good material to work on, and two out of every three of his characters were in all probability drawn from life. George Eliot in her early books, and even in *Felix Holt*, has drawn specimens of the illiterate class who talk theology like the Bench of Bishops—except that they are all Dissenters—and politics like the young Radicals who sit, or used to sit, below the gangway. But the reader felt that the author had seen these rustic theologians and politicians and heard their conversations. Shakspeare also has his metaphysical clowns ready by force of mother-wit to discuss generalities on most subjects. But neither his clowns, nor George Eliot's rustics, nor Scott's peasants, rise to anything like the flights of abstract reasoning with which Mr. Hardy credits his cider-drinking boors. . . .

The Times, 25 January 1875

Mr. Hardy showed signs last year, in 'A Pair of Blue Eyes,' of having raised for himself a higher standard of excellence than that with which ordinary novel-writers and ordinary novel-readers are well content. In his new book, 'Far from the Madding Crowd' (2 vols., Smith and Elder), there is still further evidence of his possessing a certain vein of original thought, and a delicate perceptive faculty, which transforms, with skilful touch, the matter-of-fact prosaic details of every-day life into an idyl or a pastoral poem. In parts this story rises to the dignity of both an idyl and a pastoral, for while some pages describe the simple life of farm and field with all the incidents of seed-time and harvest, reaping and shearing, there are other passages in which Mr. Hardy deals with the subtle promptings of a wilful woman's heart, or with the strong, fervent love of a grown man, and which yet are as unconventional and true to nature as his description of the quiet slopes of Norcombe Hill. This idyllic or romantic element is never violent or forced, and is always kept within due bounds. Though the book is rich in fancy, imagination never gains an undue mastery over the writer; there is the comfortable sense all the time that Mr. Hardy has his subject well in hand, and, for all its tragic tendencies, will never let it turn to ranting or pathos. Praise is so pleasant and appropriate in noticing this book that it is necessary not to lose sight of, or merge in compliment, the observation which will force itself upon the most friendly critic. It is that almost from the first page to the last the reader is never quite free from a suspicion—which at times swells into certainty—that Mr. Hardy is, consciously or unconsciously, imitating George Eliot's phraseology and style of dealing with the rough material of words. . . .

[FREDERICK NAPIER BROOME]

The Guardian, 24 February 1875

. . . It is in truth a purely pastoral idyll, in which, however, the shepherds and shepherdesses are of a very different strain from the Corydon and Phillis of conventional poetry. They are down-right farm labourers, heavy, and slow, and somewhat gross, but with touches of awkward humour and a certain sententious method of talk, which is often exceedingly amusing. These occupy the whole ground, so to speak, of the picture, and even the more prominent figures which are projected upon it rise no higher in the scale of society than farmers or farmers' daughters, and, in one important instance, a Sergeant of the Dragoon Guards. But every one of these figures is perfect, solid, and substantial, with a distinct individuality of his own, so that it would be almost possible to assign every speech to its proper speaker without looking at the name. The only exception perhaps to this lies in the hero, Gabriel Oak, a shepherd smitten with hopeless love for his mistress, Bathsheba Everdene, a young woman of manifold attractions but skittish propensities, who is excellently drawn. Oak's love is rather too high-toned for the general pitch of the work, and Oak himself rises somewhat too much above the class he lives amongst; but a hero is necessary in order to produce a story, and it is always difficult to create a hero, when the real interest of the book lies rather in his surroundings than in himself. . . .

❡ *The Spectator* greeted the very first instalment of *Far from the Madding Crowd* with the suggestion that it was by George Eliot. Hardy himself was surprised at this, and Leslie Stephen wrote to him:

I am glad to congratulate you on the reception of your first number. Besides the gentle *Spectator*, which thinks that you must be George Eliot because you know the names of the stars, several good judges have spoken to me warmly of the *Madding Crowd* . . .

The true authorship was soon known, but the suggestion stuck: and a large number of reviewers (not only those included here), after agreeing that it was plausible, went on to say that nonetheless the book was not *really* like George Eliot. *The Figaro* (not here included) said that its description of the rustics and their talk was not nearly as accurate as hers: the reviewer claimed 'a long acquaintance with the rustic life described by both these authors', and said that George Eliot was never mistaken, whereas there were 'numerous slips, or exaggerations, in the work of Mr. Hardy'. Others (like *The Examiner*) said that it had not her mastery of language, and several found Hardy guilty of a form of authorial intrusion more indirect, but more damaging, than hers: this is clearest in Hutton's complaint in *The Spectator* that Hardy blends his own thoughts with the consciousness of his characters. We can see how widespread the mistake had been from the tone of *The Observer*'s opening paragraph: contemptuous of the ascription to George Eliot, this reviewer nonetheless cannot stop thinking about it, and is even willing to use Hardy as a stick to beat her with.

The reviewer from the New York *Nation* is included for the sake of the reviewer. Henry James naturally writes with intelligence and charm, though in the same leisurely polysyllables, the same cultivated, mildly ironic, tone, that can be found in a dozen other reviewers. I wonder how many readers could have picked this out as being by James. Perhaps only one sentence has his inimitable touch: 'Everything human in the book strikes us as factitious and insubstantial; the only things we believe in are the sheep and the dogs.' Yet how much more significance even a mundane article like this takes on if we place it in the context of a great writer's work, and see it as part of the development of his opinions. It is interesting to know that James thought so well of Charles Reade, or believed that novels had better be kept short so as to win out in the struggle for existence (cultural Darwinism is everywhere in the mid-nineteenth century!). Interesting, too, that his admiration for Hardy was so lukewarm—as we shall see again later.

There was little agreement when it came to particular characters. James objected to Bathsheba; but *The Echo* (not here included) found Bathsheba, the 'winning and wayward heroine', to be the author's masterpiece. On the book as a whole the critics were more agreed, and they all liked its pastoral, idyllic quality. The story of *Far from the Madding Crowd* could, after all, be the story of a ballad: the soldier lover, the betrayed maiden, the neglected wife, the faithful shepherd, the aloof, tormented gentleman lover. This is its limitation but also its charm—even, in a quaint way, its integrity.

Gabriel Oak is the earliest of the line of Hardy heroes—Giles Winterborne and Diggory Venn are the others—who represent the rural community's own best self, its point of articulateness: Gabriel is the good shepherd they all try, fitfully and inadequately, to be. This, of course, poses an artistic problem: he must be different from the other rustics, but not too different. *The Guardian* clearly felt that he *was* too different, his love 'too high-toned', his character rising 'somewhat too much above the class he lives amongst'. This is partly true: yet the real truth is, perhaps, slightly different. The serious discrepancy is not that between Oak and his environment, but between the Oak of the opening chapters (viewed by the author with the same amused condescension as Joseph Poorgrass) and the Oak who later rises to his full role as hero, when Hardy finds that 'a hero is necessary in order to produce a story'.

Far from the Madding Crowd produced, as far as we know, the first study of Hardy in French—an article by Léon Boucher in *La Revue des Deux Mondes* for 15 December 1875, entitled 'le Roman pastoral en Angleterre'. None of Hardy's novels had yet been translated into French. The first, oddly enough, was *The Trumpet-Major* in 1882, followed by *Far from the Madding Crowd* (under the title *Barbara*), *Tess* and *Jude*, all in 1901.

Boucher's article is undistinguished but laudatory. *Far from the Madding Crowd*, then Hardy's most recent novel, is his favourite:

'Le succès, si grand qu'il ait été, est peut-être resté inférieur au mérite.' The great merit of the book, he claims, is its rejuvenation of 'le genre antique et souvent ennuyeux de la pastorale'. Most English novelists give us too much enthusiastic nature description:

> Au moindre buisson couvert de chèvrefeuille ou d'aubépine, au moindre mur revêtu de lierre, au moindre chêne seigneurial, ce sont des extases sans fin, des dithyrambes interminables: le chêne ne manque jamais de remonter à la conquête normande, et le lierre amène avec lui tout le cortège des souvenirs d'enfance et de famille ... Dire simplement les choses nouvelles, et donner aux choses simples une expression neuve, c'est là un vieux précepte que plus d'un devrait méditer. M. Hardy le connaît, et, ce qui est mieux encore, il le pratique. Il aime la nature, mais il ne s'amuse pas à la décrire longuement.

In his last paragraph, Boucher points out Hardy's fondness for psychological analysis (not carried to extremes), calls him a realist, 'mais à sa manière, avec une nuance de rêverie pleine de grace', and ends with a speculation on his future career:

> Il ne rencontrera peut-être plus souvent de sujet aussi heureux que celui qu'il vient de traiter, car il y a certaines œuvres dont on n'est capable qu'une fois; mais ceux qui aiment à trouver dans le romancier un véritable écrivain sauront lui faire une place à part et le distinguer dans la foule.

As we look through the reviews of Hardy's other novels, we find that each of them, as it was praised, was held to be not so good as *Far from the Madding Crowd*, which, the *Westminster Review* wrote in 1883, 'is, on the whole, perhaps the finest, as it is certainly the most popular among Mr. Hardy's other novels'. Reading these later (often favourable) reviews, we get the impression that *Far from the Madding Crowd* was received with much more enthusiasm than was in fact the case. It may be that the reviewers projected their disappointment with later books into a flattering distortion of what they had thought of the earlier one; it may simply be that the novel improved in memory, or on re-reading.

4 · THE RETURN
OF THE NATIVE

❡ *The Return of the Native* was probably written during 1877 and part of 1878. Leslie Stephen turned it down for the *Cornhill*, and it was serialised in *Belgravia*, January–December 1878, and in *Harper's New Monthly Magazine*, in America, February 1878–January 1879. It was published on 4 November 1878 by Smith Elder and Co., and in America shortly afterwards, by Henry Holt. The English edition was not a great success; a few copies were remaindered.

Letter from Thomas Hardy to Arthur
Hopkins, the illustrator

... The order of importance of the characters is as follows—1 Clym Yeobright, 2 Eustacia, 3 Thomasin and the reddleman, 4 Wildeve, 5 Mrs Yeobright. ...

The Athenaeum, 23 November 1878

Where are we to turn for a novelist? Mr. Black having commanded success, appears to be in some little danger of allowing his past performances to remain his chief title to deserving it; and now Mr. Hardy, who at one time seemed as promising as any of the younger generation of story-tellers, has published a book distinctly inferior to anything of his which we have yet read. It is not that the story is ill-conceived—on the contrary, there are the elements of a good novel in it; but there is just that fault which would appear in the pictures of a person who has a keen eye for the picturesque without having learnt to draw. One sees what he means, and is all the more disappointed at the clumsy way in which the meaning is expressed. People talk as no people ever talked before, or perhaps we should rather say as no people ever talk now. The language of his peasants may be Elizabethan, but it can hardly be Victorian. Such phrases as 'being a man of the mournfullest make, I was scared a little,' or 'he always had his great indignation ready against anything underhand,' are surprising in the mouth of the modern rustic. Indeed, the talk seems pitched throughout in too high a key to suit the talkers. A curious feature in the book is the low social position of the characters. The upper rank is represented by a young man who is assistant to a Paris jeweller, an innkeeper who has served his apprenticeship to a civil engineer, the daughter of a bandsman, and two or three of the small farmer class. These people all speak in a manner suggestive of high cultivation, and some of them intrigue almost like dwellers in Mayfair, while they live on nearly equal terms with the furze-cutting rustics who form a chorus reminding one of 'On ne badine pas avec l'amour.' All this is mingled with a great deal of description, showing a keen observation of natural things, though disfigured at times by forced allusions and images. The sound of reeds in a wind is likened to 'sounds as of a congregation praying humbly.' A girl's recollections 'stand like gilded uncials upon the dark tablet of her present surroundings.' The general plot of the story turns on the old theme of a man who is in love with two women, and a woman who is in love with two men; the man and the woman being both selfish and sensual. We use the last word in its more extended sense; for there is nothing in the book to provoke a comparison with the vagaries of some recent novelists, mostly of the gentler sex. But one cannot help seeing that the two persons in question know no other law than the gratification of their own passion, although this is not carried to a point which would place the book on the 'Index' of respectable households. At the same time it is clear that Eustacia Vye belongs essentially to the class of which Madame Bovary is the type; and it is impossible not to regret, since this is a type which English opinion will not allow a novelist to depict in its completeness, that Mr. Hardy should have wasted his powers in giving what after all is an imperfect and to some extent misleading view of it.

The Athenaeum, 30 November 1878
Dialect in Novels

A somewhat vexed question is reopened in your criticism of my story, 'The Return of the Native'; namely, the representation in writing of the speech of the peasantry when that writing is intended to show mainly the character of the speakers, and only to give a general idea of their linguistic peculiarities.

An author may be said to fairly convey the spirit of intelligent peasant talk if he retains the idiom, compass, and characteristic expressions, although he may not encumber the page with obsolete pronunciations of the purely English words, and with mispronunciations of those derived from Latin and Greek. In the printing of standard speech hardly any phonetic principle at all is observed; and if a writer attempts to exhibit on paper the precise accents of a rustic speaker he disturbs the proper balance of a true representation by unduly insisting upon the grotesque element; thus directing attention to a point of inferior interest, and diverting it from the speaker's meaning, which is by far the chief concern where the aim is to depict the men and their natures rather than their dialect forms.   THOMAS HARDY

The Academy, 30 November 1878

... The story is a sad one; but the sadness is unnecessary and uncalled for. A chapter of accidents makes the hero seem to cast off his mother, who thereupon dies; a second chapter of accidents sends the heroine to death by drowning. And the hero, burdened with a double remorse, is left to live on, and to take what is substantially the place in the world that he had desired ere destruction came upon him. It is all very mournful, and very cruel, and very French; and to those who have the weakness of liking to be pleasantly interested in a book it is also very disagreeable. Perhaps, too, it is false art; but of that, believing Mr. Hardy to have a very complete theory about his books, I will not speak. To me, however, nearly all that is best in the novel is analytic and descriptive. I know of nothing in later English so striking and on the whole so sound as the several pictures of Egdon Heath, or the introductory analysis of the character of Eustacia Vye. In these Mr. Hardy is seen at his best and strongest. Acute, prescient, imaginative, insatiably observant, and at the same time so rigidly and so finely artistic that there is scarce a point in the whole that can be fairly questioned, he seems to me to paint the woman and the place as no other living writer could have done. Whether he makes the best use of them afterwards need not be here discussed. ...

The Spectator, 8 February 1879

... The book, which is meant to be tragic in its gloom, and would assuredly be tragic but for a tendency, which we attribute to the sombre fatalism of the author, to lower appreciably below the truth

the whole tone and significance of human destiny, treats tragedy
itself as hardly more than a deeper tinge of the common leaden-
colour of the human lot, and so makes it seem less than tragedy,—
drearness, rather than tragedy,—by making human passion in
general commonplace and poor. . . . Tragedy is almost impossible
to people who feel and act as if they were puppets of a sort of fate.
Tragedy gives us the measure of human greatness, and elevates us
by giving it in the very moment when we sound the depth of human
suffering. Mr. Hardy's tragedy seems carefully limited to gloom. It
gives us the measure of human miserableness, rather than of
human grief,—of the incapacity of man to be great in suffering,
or anything else, rather than of his greatness in suffering. The
death of Mrs. Yeobright,—the mother of the hero,—is gloom in its
deepest intensity; and even her son's excruciating self-reproaches,
though they at least have plenty of remorse in them, are too little
softened by religious feeling or anything else to express anything
but misery. Mr. Hardy refuses to give us what, even without any
higher world of feeling, would have raised this alienation of mother
and son into tragedy,—the mutual recognition of mother and son,
and the recognition of their misunderstanding, before her death.
The hero's agony is pure, unalloyed misery, not grief of the deepest
and noblest type, which can see a hope in the future and repent the
errors of the past. And so it is with the other features of the tale.
Eustacia's inability to tell whether she really loves her husband or
not, whether she really loves Wildeve or not, and Wildeve's
inability to tell whether he really loves his wife or not,—whether
his passion for Eustacia is nothing but jealousy of another man,—
and the death which overtakes them both when on a doubtful
errand, concerning which neither of them is quite certain whether
it is to be innocent or not,—all these are characteristics of a
peculiar imaginative mood,— a mood in which there seems to be
no room for freedom, no great heights, no great depths in human
life, only the ups and downs of a dark necessity, in which men play
the parts of mere offsprings of the physical universe, and are
governed by forces and tides no less inscrutable. . . .

[? R. H. HUTTON]

❦ There was a certain disappointment over *The Return of the
Native*—together with some retrospective praise of *Far from the
Madding Crowd*. Even *The Spectator*, in its favourable notice ('a
story of singular power and interest . . . and from beginning to end
in the highest degree vivid'), took Hardy to task for never rising
to true tragedy, for treating 'tragedy itself as hardly more than a

deeper tinge of the common leaden-colour of the human lot'. Expanding this judgment towards the end of the article, the critic elaborates his theory of tragedy together with his criticisms of the novel, and we have given this passage. *The Times* wrote less on the story than on the setting, and with less than usual enthusiasm ('we can scarcely get up a satisfactory interest in people whose history and habits are so entirely foreign to our own'). Several critics saw Hardy as clever: 'It is all very mournful, and very cruel, and very French,' said *The Academy*, and claimed that his books were valuable 'rather as the outcome of a certain mind than as studies in human nature'. So too *The Saturday Review*, in its discussion of whether it is better for a novelist to be clever or entertaining, Hardy being cited as an example of the former. (This discussion, though it begins a review of *The Return of the Native*, seemed to us better placed in the general section, and will be found on page 153). Hardy's cleverness, however, is not at all incompatible with the naïvety which made Henry James refer to him as 'the good little Thomas Hardy' (see page 85). Hardy theorises with an often awkward earnestness that might belong to his own heroes and heroines. Hence the clumsiness, the heavy laboriousness, that sometimes disfigures his novels and hence, too, much of their peculiar charm. There were some advantages in being a bucolic Schopenhauer.

Only one critic considered *The Return of the Native* Hardy's best novel: Lionel Johnson, in his study *The Art of Thomas Hardy*, published in 1894.

We have included the *Athenaeum* notice not only for his own sake, but also because of the reply it drew from Hardy himself. Hardy was clearly aware of the problems of using dialect and perhaps rather defensive about his policy. Three years later he wrote to *The Spectator* (15 October 1881) on the same subject. He had been accused of writing 'whole conversations which are, to the ordinary reader, nothing but a series of linguistic puzzles'. In reply, he said:

. . . So much has my practice been the reverse of this (as a glance at my novels will show) that I have been reproved for too freely translating dialect-English into readable English, by those of your contemporaries who attach more importance to the publication of local niceties of speech than I do. The rule of scrupulously preserving the local idiom, together with the words which have no synonym among those in general use, while printing in the ordinary way most of those local expressions which are but a modified articulation of words in use elsewhere, is the rule I naturally follow. . . .

A final paragraph shows his affection for dialect, regretting (in quaintly Darwinian language) this cavalier treatment of

varieties of English which are intrinsically as genuine, grammatical and worthy of the royal title as is the all-prevailing competitor which bears it; whose only fault was that they happened not to be central, and therefore were worsted in the struggle for existence, when a uniform tongue became a necessity among the advanced classes of the population. . . .

Like most of Hardy's novels, *The Return of the Native* was first published as a serial; and like *Tess*, it was altered to please the magazine-reading public. But unlike *Tess*, it was not altered back again. Hardy stated in 1912 that 'the original conception of the story did not design a marriage between Thomasin and Venn. . . . But certain circumstances of serial publication led to a change of intent.' We do not know if this refers to the English serialisation, in *Belgravia*, or the American, in *Harper's Magazine*.

5 · THE MAYOR
OF CASTERBRIDGE

❲ *The Mayor of Casterbridge* was written during 1884, and finished on 17 April 1885. It was published serially in *The Graphic* from 2 January to 15 May 1886, and in book form by Smith Elder and Co. on 10 May 1886. In America it was serialised in *Harper's Weekly* and published, at much the same time as the English edition, by Henry Holt. The serial version was considerably revised (not simply unbowdlerised) for book publication. Like its predecessor, it was not a great success, and a few copies were remaindered.

The Saturday Review, 29 May 1886

It is small dispraise of Mr. Hardy's novel *The Mayor of Casterbridge* to say that it is not equal to the author's great and most picturesque romance of rural life, *Far From the Madding Crowd*. Nevertheless, *The Mayor of Casterbridge* is a disappointment. The story, which is very slight and singularly devoid of interest, is, at the same time, too improbable. It is fiction stranger than truth; for, even at the comparatively distant date—some fifty years ago—and in the remote region—which we are unable to localize—when and where the scenes are laid, it is impossible to believe that the public sale by a husband of his wife and child to a sailor, in a crowded booth at a village fair, could have attracted such slight attention from the many onlookers, that the newly-assorted couple should have been able to walk off and disappear so entirely within a few hours, and that the vendor on coming to his senses the following morning, repenting him of the evil, and perhaps thinking that 5*l.* was too small a price for a good-looking young woman, was unable to trace them, though he appears to have attempted the task in earnest. Again, is it possible that Michael Henchard, thoroughly selfish and unprincipled when young, could have been

4

refined by a temperance vow, and a hard-handed money-getting life, into a man of considerable delicacy, honour, and generosity? Mrs. Henchard, alias Newson, is so colourless as to be almost imperceptible. Elizabeth Jane is excellent, but rather more than a trifle dull; and unless corn-factors have hitherto been a grossly maligned race, surely Farfrae has more scruples than any corn-factor that ever lived. Are flourishing businesses established in small country towns by refusal to deal with a rival's old customers; or rather, we should say, were they *ever* thus established? No one nowadays is in the least likely to try the experiment. It is matter for regret that the author omits to publish 'Donald Farfrae's' secret recipe for turning 'grown' wheat into good wholesome bread stuff, 'restored quite enough to make good seconds out of it,' though he frankly admits that 'to fetch it back entirely is impossible. Nature won't stand so much as that.' We are inclined to think that Nature will not.

But if Mr. Hardy's narrative is not thrilling, his descriptive powers are as great as ever. Nothing can be better than his sketches of Casterbridge, the old Roman garrison town, overgrown rather than obliterated by an English *urbe in rure*. His strongest point, however, is his capacity for pourtraying the average peasant, more especially the peasant who has passed middle age. The dialect of the agricultural labourer, his ways of thought, and his mode of speech are alike admirably given. The rustic dialogue, indeed, forms the most, if not the only, amusing portion of the book. One of the best specimens which, if space permitted, we should be tempted to quote at length is the conversation between Mrs. Cuxsom and Solomon Longways, wherein village views on funeral rites are frankly set forth. With his keen insight into the character of the rural poor Mr. Hardy has not failed to notice that with them custom breeds, if not contempt of gifts and the giver, at any rate a lack of the courtesy of acknowledgment. 'Nance Mockridge,' standing with her hands on her hips, 'easefully looking at the preparations on her behalf' made by her young mistress, is drawn from the life. Equally characteristic of the country mayor who has risen from the ranks is Henchard's intolerance of his stepdaughter's natural good breeding, which prompts her to go to the kitchen instead of ringing, and persistently to thank the parlour-maid for everything she does; but for a man who cannot talk English even decently his anger at Elizabeth Jane's provincialisms is not quite so intelligible.

Another proof of how thoroughly Mr. Hardy has studied the workings of the rustic mind is given in the short account of Henchard's visit to 'Fall' or 'Wide-oh,' as he was called behind his back, a sort of mild professor of the black art, whose simple magic was secretly invoked by yokels of all classes, who nevertheless always comported themselves during the séance as it were under protest. Whenever they consulted him they did it 'for a fancy.' When they paid him they said, 'Just a trifle for 'Xmas or Candlemas,' as the case might be. The 'skimmington' or 'skimmity' ride will, we fancy, be a novelty to most readers, though the author has doubtless witnessed, or has excellent warranty for describing, this burlesque but forcible protest against what villagers regard as unseemly pre-nuptial conduct on the part of a bride. The worst feature of the book is, that it does not contain a single character capable of arousing a passing interest in his or her welfare. Even the *dramatis personæ*, with the exception of Lucetta, who conceives so sudden and violent a passion for Farfrae, are in doubt almost up to the last moment whether they really care about anybody.

The Spectator, 5 June 1886

Mr. Hardy has not given us any more powerful study than that of Michael Henchard. Why he should especially term his hero in his title-page a 'man of character,' we do not clearly understand. Properly speaking, character is the stamp graven on a man, and character therefore, like anything which can be graven, and which, when graven, remains, is a word much more applicable to that which has fixity and permanence, than to that which is fitful and changeful, and which impresses a totally different image of itself on the wax of plastic circumstance at one time, from that which it impresses on a similarly plastic surface at another time. To keep strictly to the associations from which the word 'character' is derived, a man of character ought to suggest a man of steady and unvarying character, a man who conveys very much the same conception of his own qualities under one set of circumstances, which he conveys under another. This is true of many men, and they might be called men of character *par excellence*. But the essence of Michael Henchard is that he is a man of large nature and depth of passion, who is yet subject to the most fitful influences, who can do in one mood acts of which he will never cease to repent in almost all his other moods, whose temper of heart changes many times even during the execution of the same purpose, though the same ardour, the same pride, the same wrathful magnanimity, the same inability to carry out in cool blood the angry resolve of the mood of revenge or scorn, the same hasty unreasonableness, and the same disposition to swing back to an equally hasty reasonableness, distinguish him throughout. In one very good sense, the great deficiency of Michael Henchard might be said to be in 'character.' It might well be said that with a little *more* character, with a little more fixity of mind, with a little more power of recovering *himself* when he was losing his balance, his would have been a nature of gigantic mould; whereas, as Mr. Hardy's novel is meant to show, it was a nature which ran mostly to waste. But, of course, in the larger and wider sense of the word 'character,' that sense which has less reference to the permanent definition of the stamp, and more reference to the confidence with which the varying moods may be anticipated, it is not inadmissible to call Michael Henchard a 'man of character.' Still, the words on the title-page rather mislead. One looks for the picture of a man of much more constancy of purpose, and much less tragic mobility of mood, than Michael Henchard. None the less, the picture is a very vivid one, and almost magnificent in its fullness of expression. The largeness of his nature, the unreasonable generosity and suddenness of his friendships, the depth of his self-humiliation for what was evil in him, the eagerness of his craving for sympathy, the vehemence of his impulses both for good and evil, the curious dash of stoicism in a nature so eager for sympathy, and of fortitude in one so moody and restless,—all these are lineaments which, mingled together as Mr. Hardy has mingled them, produce a curiously strong impression of reality, as well as of homely grandeur.

Our only quarrel with Mr. Hardy is that while he draws a figure which, in spite of the melancholy nature of its career and the tragic close of that career, is certainly a noble one, and one, on the whole, *more* noble in its end than in its beginning, he intersperses throughout his story hints of the fashionable pessimism, a philosophy which seems to us to have little appropriateness to the homely scenery and characters which he portrays. For example, as Mr. Hardy approaches the end of his story, he says of his hero:—

'Externally there was nothing to hinder his making another start on the upward slope, and by his new lights achieving higher things than his soul in its half-formed state had been able to accomplish. But the ingenious machinery contrived by the gods for reducing human possibilities of amelioration to a minimum— which arranges that wisdom to do shall come *pari passu* with the departure of zest for doing—stood in the way of all that. He had no wish to make an arena a second time of a world that had become a mere painted scene to him.'

To our minds, these very pagan reflections are as much out of place as they are intrinsically false. The natural and true reflection would have been that Michael Henchard, after his tragic career of passionate sin, bitter penitence, and rude reparation, having been brought to a better and humbler mind than that which had for the most part pervaded his life, the chief end of that life had been achieved, and that it mattered little in comparison whether he should or should not turn the wisdom he had acquired to the purpose of hewing out for himself a wiser and soberer career. Those who believe that the only 'human possibilities of amelioration' of any intrinsic worth, are ameliorations of the spirit of human character, cannot for a moment admit that when that has been achieved, it can add much to such an amelioration, that it should receive the sanction of a little earthly success. If life be the school of character, and if the character, once fairly schooled into a nobler type, passes from this school to another and higher school, we have no reason to complain. What Mr. Hardy calls 'the ingenious machinery contrived by the gods for reducing human possibilities of amelioration to a minimum,' appears to us to be the means taken by the moral wisdom which overrules our fate for showing us that the use of character is not to mould circumstance, but rather that it is the use of circumstance to chasten and purify character. Michael Henchard's proud and lonely death shows, indeed, that he had but half learned his lesson; but it certainly does not in any way show that the half-learned lesson had been wasted. There is a grandeur of conception about this shrewd, proud, illiterate, primitive nature, which, so far as we remember, surpasses anything which even Mr. Hardy has yet painted for us in that strong and nervous school of delineation in which he excels so much. Michael Henchard's figure should live with us as Scott's picture of Steenie Mucklebacket or David Deans lives with us. Indeed, Scott never gave to a figure of that kind so much study and such painstaking portraiture as Mr. Hardy has given to his Mayor of Casterbridge. [R. H. HUTTON]

❧ Perhaps we ought to have chosen *The Mayor of Casterbridge* for detailed treatment: many today would claim it as Hardy's masterpiece. It has a brutal power that Hardy never again equalled; and for all the absurdities of plot, its action follows an archetypal path that enabled one modern critic to analyse it, with detailed and impressive ingenuity, as a kind of Frazer-cum-Jung corn-god myth (D. A. Dike: *A Modern Oedipus*, Essays in Criticism, April

1952). Hardy regards Henchard with a cool surface detachment
all through the book, even disapproves of him: yet below this his
identification with Henchard must have been very deep and strong,
and the final chapters of this book, when Henchard is isolated and
in despair, are as moving as anything in his fiction. It was wrong
of us, surely, to give so little space to this novel, when *Far from the
Madding Crowd* and *Jude* are treated at such length.

And yet, reading the reviews, one sees that it was not wrong.
Contemporary criticism of *The Mayor of Casterbridge* was not very
interesting. Everyone at the time preferred *Far from the Madding
Crowd*, and even those who enjoyed *The Mayor* do not always seem
to have responded to its peculiar greatness. *The Guardian* found it
'worth reading, though it is not a pleasant book', and went on to
make the usual complaint about the 'dreary impression' it left:
'its outlook is narrow, its tone is prosaic, and its last word is
elaborately pessimistic'. *The Westminster Review* did say 'the
character of Henchard is a grand study which has not, so far as we
recollect, its prototype in fiction'; but that is all it said, in a brief
(though enthusiastic) notice of the novel among dozens of others.
Several reviewers continued to praise 'Hardy's capacity for portraying the average peasant' (*The Saturday Review*), and even
those who concentrated on the character of Henchard had reservations. *The Spectator* (above) queried the description of him as a
man of character. It is difficult to be sure, reading the first paragraph, if this is a mere quibble over terms ('in the larger and
wider sense of the word "character" . . . it is not inadmissible to
call Michael Henchard a "man of character"'), or a genuinely
different conception of human nature. Reading on, we see it to be
the latter. In rebuking Hardy's fatalism, and substituting something nearer a moral conception of character and action, the critic
is making a legitimate point—yet (perhaps) a point that would
prevent anyone who accepted it from creating a Michael Henchard.

6 · THE WOODLANDERS

❡ *The Woodlanders* was written at Max Gate, Hardy's Dorchester house; it was begun towards the end of 1885, and finished 4 February 1887. Hardy submitted two titles to Macmillan, who chose the present one (the other was 'Fitzpiers at Hintock'). It was published serially in *Macmillan's Magazine*, May 1886–April 1887, and in *Harper's Bazaar*, in America, 15 May 1886–9 April 1887. It was published in book form by Macmillan on 15 March 1887, and in America by Harper in the same year—the end of Hardy's long association with Henry Holt.

The Spectator, 26 March 1887

This is a very powerful book, and as disagreeable as it is powerful. It is a picture of shameless falsehood, levity, and infidelity, followed by no true repentance, and yet crowned at the end with perfect success; nor does Mr. Hardy seem to paint his picture in any spirit of indignation that redeems the moral drift of the book. He does not impress us as even personally disposed to resent the good-natured profligacy of his hero; and the letter which Fitzpiers sends his wife towards the close of the story,—the letter which opens the way to the renewal of their married life,—has in it an unashamed air, by which Grace, if she had been all that Mr. Hardy wishes us to believe her, would have been more revolted than gratified. On the whole, Mr. Hardy has painted nothing more thoroughly disagreeable than this mendacious, easy-going, con-scienceless, passionate young doctor, with his fastidious selfishness and his scientific acuteness, and his aristocratic self-esteem, availing himself of the weakness of every woman for whom he feels the least fancy, and almost more attracted at the close by his mistaken belief in his wife's infidelity to him, than he was at first by her purity and innocence. Mr. Hardy's story is written with an indifference to the moral effect it conveys of which we have found distinct traces before in his books, especially in *Ethelberta's Hand*, but which, in our opinion, lowers the art of his works quite as much as it lowers their moral tone. It is impossible to admire Giles Winterborne and Marty South as Mr. Hardy intends us to admire them, without also feeling indignation and disgust towards Fitzpiers which Mr. Hardy not only does not express, but even renders it impossible for us to suppose that he entertains. And this affects the whole story, and makes us regard it with a sort of dislike that is most unfavourable to a work of art, the dislike which springs from the feeling that the artist has not truly estimated the significance of his own work. A more unworthy and godless creature than Fitzpiers to find favour, as he evidently does, in the mind of the artist who painted his likeness, it would not be easy to discover in our modern fiction; and though he is well drawn, he is drawn with an air of something like apology, if not sympathy, that sends a discordant vibration through the whole tale. Mr. Hardy will say that in painting Winterborne, he has given the standard by which to try Fitzpiers and find him wanting, which would be true, if only there were not a vein of positive liking for him that penetrates the tale, and annuls all the effect of Winterborne's faithfulness, manliness, and pure disinterestedness. It is evident, for instance, at the close of the tale, that Mr. Hardy spares Fitzpiers the man-trap which the vindictiveness of Tim Tangs had prepared for him, and even turns it into the means of reconciling him to his wife, from a feeling of tenderness for him which we cannot admire. We will admit that there is no case for what used to be called 'poetical justice' in novels. It is quite true that there is but little of it in real life, except the rewards and punishments which the conscience itself bestows. The man-trap, even if Fitzpiers had been caught in it, might have done him no moral good, though to have been nursed by his wife in the pain and mutilation which it would have inflicted on him, would have been too good a fate for his deserts. But even putting aside the wish so commonly felt for what is called poetical justice, Mr. Hardy ought not to have allowed this sensual and selfish liar, good-natured in an easy way though he certainly was, to be received back into his wife's favour and made happy on terms so easy as are here imposed on him. . . .

[R. H. HUTTON]

❡ There is nothing new to record in the reception of *The Woodlanders*. Once again, the rural setting and the minor characters received most praise; once again, the book was considered powerful but disagreeable. *The Academy* found it his best book since *Far from the Madding Crowd*, but predicted that nine out of ten readers

would dislike it. *The Guardian* (like most modern readers) gave the
highest praise to the characters of Giles Winterborne and Marty
South; unlike most modern readers, it objected to 'the utterly
needless introduction of coarse and repulsive incidents'. *The
Westminster Review* was (as usual) brief and favourable. *The
Saturday Review* found Giles a little too idealised, 'a little too consciously treated as the incarnation of a phase of village civilisation,
and not quite enough as an individual'. Hutton in *The Spectator*
made the same complaint as he had made in the case of *The Mayor
of Casterbridge*, that there was not sufficient moral element in the
portrayal of human nature. The case is stated more crudely this
time: he rebukes Hardy for not feeling any 'spirit of indignation',
and despite his disclaimer he does seem to be asking for something
very like poetic justice. There is no sign of the kind of enthusiasm
felt, for instance, by Arnold Bennett, who said that if he had to
choose the finest English novel he would undoubtedly choose *The
Woodlanders*.

7 · TESS OF
THE D'URBERVILLES

❡ *Tess* was certainly begun by August 1889, and possibly as early
as the autumn of 1888; it is not known when it was finished. It was
first offered to Tillotson and Son of Bolton, who had a newspaper
syndicate, and wished to serialise it; they had set some of it up in
type before they realised what the book was like, and then
declined it. Hardy never mentioned this episode, which took place
in August–September 1889. It was then turned down by *Murray's
Magazine* in October, and by *Macmillan's Magazine* in November.
Hardy then set out, more or less cynically, to truncate it in order
to make it fit for serial publication, and it appeared in *The Graphic*,
with some chapters omitted and a little local bowdlerising, from
4 July to 26 December 1891. Some of the omitted parts were
published separately, with the names of the characters removed
so that it was not clear that they came from *Tess*. One of these,
called 'The Midnight Baptism, a Study in Christianity', appeared
in the *Fortnightly* in May 1891, and was thus the first piece of the
novel to be published. The seduction of Tess was printed under the
title 'Saturday Night in Arcady' in a literary supplement of the
National Observer of Edinburgh, 14 November 1891. The *Graphic*
version was also serialised in *Harper's Bazaar* from 18 July to 26
December 1891.

Tess was published in three volumes, with the deletions restored,
by Osgood, McIlvaine and Co. in November 1891; and in 1892 by
Harper in America.

Hardy tells something of this story in the explanatory note to
the first edition of the book; and discusses its reception in his very
interesting *Preface* to the fifth edition.

Tess brought Hardy both fame and money on a scale he had
never known before. Something of the fame is shown in the pages

that follow; the money was due not only to its wide sales, but to the passing of the International Copyright Law in America in 1891. It was the first of Hardy's novels to be published under the new law, which protected English authors for the first time against piracy in America, and thus ended a long and bitter grievance going back at least to the time of Dickens's first visit to New York.

The Speaker, 26 December 1891

Mr. Hardy's latest novel will certainly take rank with the best productions of his pen. It deals with the old country, the old scenes, and, we might almost say, the old people. The Wessex peasantry are once more brought upon the stage, and the dignity, the tragedy, the comedy of their lives are again presented to us. There is no single person in the book whose rank is higher than that of the middle-class; and the few people of education and comparatively fair means who figure in it are the exceptions to the rule. It is the lives of the toilers that Mr. Hardy paints, with the minuteness, the loving care, the sympathy, the instinctive rightness which characterise genius. Never has he drawn a sweeter heroine than the girl whose story concerns us here. Yet though she is one of the people, bound to earn her living by the strength of her hands and the sweat of her brow, she is in one respect distinguished from most of Mr. Hardy's former heroines. Her father, John Durbyfield, though a mere peasant, is the last survivor of an ancient race, the d'Urbervilles, who once owned great estates in Wessex, and lorded it over their neighbours. Whether Mr. Hardy has sought in this story to show the consequences of the heroine's strain of aristocratic blood in her life as a peasant, we can hardly pretend to say. If this has been his intention, he has been careful not to obtrude it upon his readers. Here and there, however, at fateful moments in the girl's life, we are brought face to face with a certain subtlety of motive on her part which seems out of keeping with the character of an ordinary farm labourer. Her physical beauty comes from her mother, the descendant of a long line of peasants. It is only in her mental attributes that we can find any trace of the d'Urbervilles of old times. We have said that, as a heroine, Tess will compare with any in Mr. Hardy's noble gallery. From the first moment at which she appears before us the reader is drawn towards her. But it is only after he has followed her through the greater part of her wanderings, in good report and evil, that he fully learns to know and love her. When he has finished the recital of her story, she is no longer the mere creation of the novelist's fancy, but a creature of flesh and blood, with noble instincts, high principles, and human infirmities, who appeals to us alike by her virtue and her misfortunes.

All this simply means that Mr. Hardy has succeeded once more in the most difficult of all the tasks which the writer of fiction can attempt—the portraiture of a living woman. With what care, by what subtle touches, and with what absolute completeness that portrait is painted for us, only those who read the story can know. It is a work of genius, such a work as could hardly have come from the pen of any other living writer. And whilst throughout the three volumes the figure of the heroine dominates all others, the background of the story is sketched in Mr. Hardy's happiest manner. Never have his peasants been more real, never have we had a keener insight into their joys and their sorrows than here. There are whole chapters of the book so steeped in the sunny atmosphere of Wessex that the reader feels himself to be one of the personages of whom Mr. Hardy writes, falls to their level and sympathises with them in their wants and woes as though he were himself to the manner born. From all this it will be seen that the admirers of Mr. Hardy will find nothing to disappoint them in 'Tess of the d'Urbervilles.' Wit and humour, pathos and sympathy, the comedy and the tragedy of life are all here; and with such surpassing skill is the work accomplished, that long after the book has been laid aside we find ourselves still living among its characters and pondering over the problems of their existence. Indeed, we hardly remember any one of Mr. Hardy's many novels which so bites into the heart and the mind of the reader as this does, making an impression upon both that can never be effaced.

We have spoken of the comedy of the story; but from the first page to the last the sombre cloud of a great tragedy hangs over it. Nothing could be more unfair to such an artist as Mr. Hardy than to tell his plot in bald outline. One has, indeed, but to recall 'Two on a Tower' in order to see how unjust it would be to the author to present to the reader the dry bones of one of his living fictions, and in no case would it have been more unfair than in the present. But it is necessary, in dealing with 'Tess of the d'Urbervilles,' to touch upon its central point. Mr. Hardy has called his story that of 'a pure woman;' and no one will lay aside the book without feeling that he has rightly described it—though the purity of the heroine is not incompatible with a grievous fall, and with misfortunes which in everyday life, and in society as it is now constituted, would have made her an outcast. Clearly it has been the purpose of the author to present the ever-recurring problem of social conduct to us in a new aspect. He sees poor Tess, amid her temptations and her despair, with 'larger, other eyes than ours,' and he seeks to make us see her in the same light. In all this he has done well, and the book is none the less valuable or the less to be praised because it is a daring and brilliant presentment of one side of the most difficult of our social problems. But where we have to remonstrate with the author is in the inexorable following of Fate which has distinguished his treatment of the subject. Never once does he falter as he leads his heroine from sorrow to sorrow, making her drink to the last drop of the cup of suffering. He is as remorseless as Fate itself in unfolding the drama of her life. Again and again the reader puts down the book, pained and almost horrified, as he sees the young girl whom he has learned to love being drawn deeper and deeper into the vortex of ruin. But an irresistible fascination compels him to take it up again and to pursue the story to the bitter end. It is a wonderful triumph of art which Mr. Hardy has given us. In many respects it is the noblest of all his presentments of a human soul. It is powerful and valuable as a contribution to the ethical education of the world. And yet the mere human reader, who knows of the sorrows around him, who may even do what in him lies to relieve those sorrows, but who would fain dwell in a brighter world than that of everyday life, cannot but utter a protest against the unredeemed sadness of this story, the lurid characters in which the dealings of fate with poor Tess of the d'Urbervilles are inscribed, the anguish and the horror in which her young life comes to its appointed close. The critic must take the work of genius as he finds it, and be grateful for it, in whatever shape it is offered to him. Nor can anyone who reads this book profess to say that at this point or at that the author would have done well to turn aside from his set purpose and to change the fate of his characters. Nay, the irresistible feeling is borne in upon the mind as one reads, that thus, and thus only, could the life of Tess Durbyfield have shaped itself; that when once she had suffered in her innocent youth the cruel wrong which changed her whole career, no other end was open to her than that which she ultimately reached. But the pity of it, and the horror, are all the greater for that very reason; and one can but hope that in his next work Mr. Hardy will find a theme not less inspiring, but infinitely more bright.

The Daily Chronicle, 28 December 1891

Mr. Thomas Hardy's new novel is as pitiless and tragic in its intensity as the old Greek dramas. Not Æschylus himself nor any of his brethren, who so rigidly illustrated the doctrine of human fate, could have woven a web that should more completely enmesh a human soul than Mr. Hardy has done in the case of his heroine, Teresa Durbeyfield, or Tess of the D'Urbervilles. What does the novelist intend to teach by this creation? Tess's life story is powerfully placed before us, and with intuitions of real genius, but its purport is to the last degree painful. It would almost seem as though the novelist believed that humanity only existed 'to be, and to do, and to suffer.' No doubt there are men and women who seem to be dogged by the footsteps of a sinister Fate from the cradle to the grave, but this pagan idea of environment surely only embraces a minority and not the majority of the human race.

The latest direct representatives of the D'Urbervilles—one of the most ancient families in Wessex—are a small farmer and his family, named Durbeyfield, living in the Vale of Blakemore or Blackmoor. The farmer and his wife lead the common, sordid, sensual lives of their order, but their daughter Tess seems to have inherited the beauty and grace of her distinguished ancestors. She is seen and coveted by a reputed D'Urberville who has no right to the name, and she falls and loses her honour. Our quarrel with Mr. Hardy respecting his heroine is that although she does not love her seducer, and indeed has before repulsed him, she easily falls into the snare. There seems no overwhelming necessity for her ruin, which is the turning-point for all the troubles that follow. A child was born, which died, and Tess's betrayer passed for a time out of her existence. After a while she was persistently wooed by a worthy young fellow, Angel Clare, the unorthodox son of a country rector. He gave her no rest until she married him, and the poor girl in vain sought for an opportunity of unburdening herself to her lover before marriage. It was only afterwards that he learnt the terrible story, and though he had himself confessed to a *liaison*, he had no pity for his wife. As the author remarks, 'the woman pays' in these cases, and very unjust it is that it should always be so. Tess loved Clare with every fibre of her being, but he went off to the Brazils to think out what the future must be. Surely never were more touching or pathetic letters written than those which Tess sent to her husband, imploring him to come back and to save her from her original tempter, who had again found her out. D'Urberville had been converted from his evil ways, and went about preaching in the villages, but as soon as he saw Tess again he flung his Christianity to the winds, assured her that Clare would never return, and so hemmed her in that she again fell, having lost all hope. Then Clare returned, and when all her misery and her love tore at her very heartstrings, she killed her betrayer D'Urberville, and suffered the legal expiation for her crime. A more appalling series of trials never fell upon a poor weak woman, and she was unable to battle with them victoriously. The tragedy of life could only end in one way with her; but her pitiful history creates a profound and sympathetic impression.

Wessex life and character have never found so graphic a delineator as in Mr. Hardy. He is as intimately at home here as Shakespeare with his creations in the Forest of Arden. He reads the nature and emotions of his *dramatis personœ* to their minutest shade. We could wish that he had selected a more pleasant subject for his latest theme, but that he treats it in a masterly manner there is no denying. Some of the dairy-farming episodes are marvellously portrayed, as are the scenes of stronger passion between Tess and her lovers, and the closing passages of all, where in her blank and utter despair at the hopelessness of life she takes swift vengeance upon her betrayer. The novel is of such a character as to haunt one long after its perusal.

Letter to *The Daily Chronicle*, 30 December 1891
The Editor of The Daily Chronicle

SIR,—There is no doubt that Mr. Hardy, in some of his recent stories, *donne un tantinet peu trop dans les noirceurs* (as our French friends would say); and that, in his latest novel, he has sounded a depth of unrelieved, relentless darkness that—with all due deference to our fogs—seems hardly in keeping with the general tendency of our Age, when 'the doctrine of human fate' does not exercise the same influence on men's minds as in the epic days of the Greek tragedians. It was not, however, to vent this remark *coram populo* that I now take up my pen, for your critic has authoritatively declared that 'a more appalling series of trials *never* fell upon a poor weak woman.' What I wish to point out is that there seems in some respects to be a remarkable resemblance between the heroine of Mr. Hardy's new novel and the heroine of a novel that was published by M. Marcel Prévost a little more than two years ago. Like Tess of the D'Urbervilles, Mademoiselle Jaufre falls an easy victim to the first beast in human form whom she meets with without loving him. Like Tess, too, Mademoiselle

Jaufre marries, and has not the courage to confess her lapse to her husband, and when she does at length unbosom herself her husband abandons her for the time, very much in the same manner (barring differing details, of course) that Tess's husband did. But here all further analogy ends. Mademoiselle Jaufre's husband is more human than Tess's, and M. Marcel Prévost's novel consequently finishes in a far more satisfactory manner than Mr. Hardy's Æschylian drama. At least, so I think. But, then, I am only,   UNE VIEILLE BADERNE

Pall Mall Gazette, 31 December 1891

This is a grim Christmas gift that Mr. Hardy makes us, in his last Wessex tale. The reader, intent on the seasonable pleasures of fiction, who carries home 'Tess of the D'Urbervilles' for his delectation over the Christmas fire, thinking perhaps to have another 'Far from the Madding Crowd,' may well feel a little shaken as the gay pastoral comedy of the opening chapters is shifted by degrees into the sombre trappings of the tragic muse. In 'Far from the Madding Crowd,' and in other of the brighter fictions of its author, there is, it is true, tragedy as well as comedy and happy endings; but the whole effect is fairly one of rustic geniality, of a residuum of happiness when all is told. Mr. Hardy here works determinedly in his most fateful vein, however—the vein of 'The Return of the Native' —with an artistic result of concentrated tragedy such as is rarely to be found in the modern novel, and such as may well make Mr. Hardy's younger contemporaries, who would write great works, despair. The art of the tale-writer who can make a simple history like that of Tess Durbeyfield (alias D'Urberville), and turn it over, and shape it, and interpret it to so profound an ethical and æsthetical result—giving it all the modern significancy you please, and yet never losing sight of the permanent, in the casual, effect, and never 'writing down' to the Philistine intelligence—is not, indeed, to be easily reduced to terms of criticism. Luckily for the validity of the present review, Mr. Hardy's art is now an old story; and it is enough to say here that he has never exercised it more powerfully—never, certainly, more tragically—than in this most moving presentment of a 'pure woman.'

. . . Here, too, enters the hero, Angel Clare, whose character (like his name—too factitious—too obviously histrionic!) is perhaps less satisfying than the simpler rustic character of Tess and her father and mother, and the other countryfolk, who are pure Wessex. Like Ibsen, Mr. Hardy does not, it is true, set out to provide us with satisfying heroes. He is fond of showing, on the contrary, how much cruelty, how much bitter suffering, your would-be hero may inflict by sticking too consistently and religiously to his role. But judged by Mr. Hardy's own standard, Angel Clare, difficult type as he is to present, is not altogether a convincing creation, especially when looked at by the side of Tess, whose verisimilitude in art and human quality is maintained throughout with a subtlety and a warm and live and breathing naturalness which one feels to be the work of a tale-teller born and not made. All the women in the book are similarly true to nature, and, what is more rare in a sense, true to art. Indeed, the book is, among great novels, peculiarly the Woman's Tragedy! It is to be only fully appreciated perhaps by a woman, in its intimate and profound interpretations of the woman's heart through the pure and beautiful and heroic Tess, doomed to many sorrows, done to death, not by slanderous tongues, but by the tyranny of man, of nature, which makes woman emotionally subject to man, and of social circumstance. . . .

Letter from George Meredith to Frederick Greenwood, 11 January 1892

Hardy is one of the few men whose work I can read. I had always great hope of him. If you will lend me his Tess, it shall be returned early.

Then, 23 February 1892:

My daughter packs and sends you' Tess' today. The work is open to criticism, but excellent and very interesting. All of the Dairy Farm held me fast. But from the moment of the meeting again of Tess and Alec, I grew cold, and should say that there is a depression of power, up to the end, save for the short scene on the plain of Stonehenge. If the author's minute method had been sustained, we should have had a finer book. It is marred by the sudden hurry to round the story. And Tess, out of the arms of Alec, into (I suppose) those of the lily necked Clare, and on to the Black Flag waving over her poor body, is a smudge in vapour—she at one time so real to me.

The Saturday Review, 16 January 1892

The sequence of lightning and thunder is not more prompt than that of cause and effect in Mr. Hardy's story. A parson riding through a country lane in the South of England meets an old haggler called Durbeyfield, and informs him that the name he bears is a corruption of D'Urberville, and that he is the 'direct lineal representative of the ancient and knightly family of the D'Urbervilles' who appear on the Battle Abbey roll. This is all news to the haggler, but he sucks it in eagerly, and listens while the parson gives—in anything but simple language—a sketch of the departed glories of his house, and he does not at all relish his informer's advice to 'do nothing.' In fact, from that very instant Durbeyfield begins 'doing' to such an extent that in the course of five years he completely *un*does, not only himself and his family, but a number of other people as well, and his own daughter Tess is the principal victim. On his way home he imparts to a boy whom he meets 'the secret that he is one of a noble race,' and that 'there's not a man in the county of South Wessex that's got grander and nobler skellingtons in his family' than he has. It is wholly beneath the dignity of such a potentate to walk home, so he sends the boy for a carriage and some rum, and drives back to his wife, repeating, as a recitative, 'I've—got—a—great—family—vault—at Kingsbere—and—knighted—forefathers—in—lead—coffins—there.' Let it at once be said that there is not one single touch of nature either in John Durbeyfield or in any other character in the book. All are stagey, and some are farcical. Tess herself comes the nearest to possibility, and is an attractive figure; but even she is suggestive of the carefully-studied simplicity of the theatre, and not at all of the carelessness of the fields. Her life is ruined by her parents' determination to send her to claim kinship with some rich people of the name of D'Urberville, who own a place about twenty miles away. Tess herself goes with extreme reluctance, and is not much prepossessed with the so-called relative that she meets, a young man of bold aspect, who regales her with strawberries. Of course this is the serpent who is to destroy the poor young Eve; but the story gains nothing by the reader being let into the secret of the physical attributes which especially fascinated him in Tess. Most people can fill in blanks for themselves, without its being necessary to put the dots on the i's so very plainly; but Mr. Hardy leaves little unsaid. 'She had an attribute which amounted to a disadvantage just now; and it was this that caused Alec D'Urberville's eyes to rivet themselves upon her. It was a luxuriance of aspect; a fulness of growth, which made her appear more of a woman than she really was. She had inherited the feature from her mother without the quality it denoted' (vol. i. p. 75). It is these side suggestions that render Mr. Hardy's story so very disagreeable, and *Tess* is full of them.

The result of this interview is that the young man induces his blind mother to offer Tess a situation as poultry-woman, and the Durbeyfield fortunes not being equal to the length of their pedigree, she is induced by her parents to accept, her mother openly declaring that she looks upon it as a chance for Tess to settle her future. Mrs. Durbeyfield is described as a good-natured shiftless woman, not refined in her perceptions, but who has led a respectable life. Yet she does not hesitate to send her daughter deliberately into temptation, with as much *sangfroid* as if she had been the vilest of her sex. 'If he don't marry her afore, he will after,' she observes to her husband (vol. i. p. 97), and he does not contradict her. The girl's ruin is compassed in spite of herself, and she comes home four months after she has first left to be upbraided by her mother for her folly in not getting D'Urberville to marry her. Tess has nothing of her mother's coarse fibre, and shrinks away from sight, till, after her baby's birth and death, she departs and seeks work in a great dairy farm. Mr. Hardy is always at his best when dealing with scenes taken direct from nature, in which his imagination has something to go upon. His description of life in a dairy farm in summer forms an admirable foil to his subsequent account of the terribly hard work both for males and females in an arable farm in winter, when swede-hacking, reed-drawing, or threshing occupied the hands from dawn to dark. It was during her easy and pleasant summer hours that Tess met her elective affinity Angel Clare, the farm pupil, son of a neighbouring clergyman. Clare is a mere shadow to the reader; but, such as he is, no less than three dairymaids sigh for him openly, while Tess does so in secret. There is a want of humour in this proceeding which is, however, intended to be tragic. 'Dear he,' as one of the forlorn ones calls him, proposes to Tess, and, after much hesitation on her part, and weak efforts to tell him her history, she marries him. On their wedding evening they resolve to confess their past sins to each other, with the consequence that, while Tess gives him, as he expects, instant absolution, Clare emphatically declines to pardon the error of which she can hardly be said to have been guilty. She has a brief revival of hope, occasioned by Clare's walking in his sleep, and performing a feat that must have been almost unique in the history of strength, considering that he was not a Hercules, and that Tess was a tall and well-developed young woman. He lifted her out of bed, murmuring tender words over his 'dead wife,' carried her out of the house, down the river across a plank bridge, through a plantation to the Abbey church, where he laid her in an open coffin, and went away. He soon went away altogether—for Brazil—giving Tess money to support her the while, and telling her that, if he could ever make up his mind to forgive her, he would come back. The end is what every one will have foreseen. Tess accidentally meets D'Urberville, who has been converted from his ways in a wholly startling manner by some warning words of Clare's father, and is now a Methodist preacher. He hangs about her, in spite of her entreaties, for many months, denies his new opinions, and offers her the marriage which is now impossible; and when, finally, Clare has decided to be magnanimous, and to claim her as his wife, he finds that it is too late, and that she is living with D'Urberville. The tragedy culminates in D'Urberville being stabbed by Tess during a quarrel, in her hiding for some days with Clare, and in her being ultimately hanged. Few people will deny the terrible dreariness of this tale, which, except during the few hours spent with cows, has not a gleam of sunshine anywhere. Mr. Hardy says in his 'explanatory note' that he has added some chapters, 'more especially addressed to adults,' to 'episodic sketches' that have appeared in various papers and periodicals. This reminds us of those artists who have exhibitions of pictures open to the public, but who hang over an inner sanctum containing their choicest works a placard marked 'For gentlemen only.' It matters much less what a story is about than how that story is told, and Mr. Hardy, it must be conceded, tells an unpleasant story in a very unpleasant way. He says that it 'represents, on the whole, a true sequence of events'; but does it? The impression of most readers will be that Tess, never having cared for D'Urberville even in her early days, hating him as the cause of her ruin, and, more so, as the cause of her separation from Clare, whom she madly loved, would have died by the roadside sooner than go back and live with him and be decked out with fine clothes. Still, Mr. Hardy did well to let her pay the full penalty, and not die among the monoliths of Stonehenge, as many writers would have done. One thing more. Mr. Hardy would do well to look to his grammar. In his 'explanatory note' he begs his too gentle reader 'who cannot endure to have it said what everybody thinks and feels,' to remember a sentence of St. Jerome's. To have *what* said? To what does 'it' refer? Then, in vol. iii. p. 198, he says:—

> The Durbeyfield waggon met many other waggons with families on the summit of a road, which was built on a well-nigh unvarying principle, as peculiar, probably, to the rural labourer as the hexagon to a bee. The groundwork of the arrangement was the family dresser.

Now, by all the rules of syntax it is the summit of the road that

was built on the unvarying principle and on the family dresser,
but the context shows that it is really the inside of the waggon to
which he means to refer. These things ought not to be.

The Spectator, 23 January 1892

Mr. Hardy has written one of his most powerful novels, perhaps
the most powerful which he ever wrote, to illustrate his conviction
that not only is there no Providence guiding individual men and
women in the right way, but that, in many cases at least, there is
something like a malign fate which draws them out of the right
way into the wrong way. Tess of the D'Urbervilles is declared by
Mr. Hardy to be 'a pure woman,' and as he has presented her, we
do not doubt that her instincts were all pure enough, more pure
probably than those of a great number of women who never fall
into her disgrace and shame. She was, of course, much more sinned
against than sinning, though Mr. Hardy is too 'faithful' a portrait-
painter to leave out touches which show that her instincts even as
regards purity, were not of the very highest class. The coarse expression which he attributes to her in relation to her companions
(Vol. I., p. 127), when she declares that if she had known what
they were like, she would not have so let herself down as to come
with them betrays perfectly well her knowledge of the dangers
before her,—indeed, she had had plenty of forecast of those dangers,
and she was well aware that the looseness of her companions was
more or less due to the profligacy of the man whom she disliked
and feared, and to whom her ruin was ultimately due. Yet she
deliberately forsook their company, because they were insolent and
taunting, to put herself into the power of the very person who, as
she knew, was responsible for their misconduct as well as for the
temptations thrown in her own way. That course was not due to an
instinct of purity, but to an instinct of mere timidity and disgust.
But though we quite admit that in her instincts Tess was as pure
as multitudes of women who never suffered what she had to suffer,
we cannot at all admit that, if she be 'faithfully presented,' she
was at all faithful to her own sense of duty in the course of the
story. Again and again, and yet again, he shows her shrinking from
the obvious and imperative duty of the moment when she must
have felt that the whole sincerity of her life was at stake. To accept
the love of her husband without telling him that she had been the
more or less innocent victim of a man to whom she had borne a
child, was not certainly the act of a 'pure woman,' and whatever
palliation there may have been for it in her passionate love, it was

the very way to ensure the steady lowering of her sense of duty, and invite the misery which was the natural consequence. But even after that, and after she had confessed to her husband, which very naturally produced a great alienation, she repeatedly shrinks from the obvious and emphatic duty of the hour, which she must have felt to be the duty enjoined by her love for him, no less than the duty enjoined by the barest self-respect. She will not stay with her parents, where she would have been comparatively safe, and where her husband had assumed that she would be safe, but goes out into all the great dangers of field-life,—dangers, we mean, for a character and beauty such as hers. When she comes to the end of her resources, and is aware that, under the terms of her husband's instructions, she ought to have applied to his father and mother for more means, she is deterred from doing so by the most trivial pride, which was natural enough, but which the sense of her general unprotectedness ought at once to have overruled. Still worse, when, on her return from this failure of purpose, she finds herself once more in the snares of the miserable man who had been her ruin, instead of at once taking refuge with her father and mother-in-law, who were her natural protectors, she trusts entirely to letters which had to go to Brazil and (as it proved) to return from Brazil, before her husband could get them, and never once thinks of repeating the application from which nothing but the least justifiable of motives had deterred her. We must say that had Tess been what Mr. Hardy calls her, a really pure woman, she could not possibly have hesitated to apply to her father and mother-in-law when she felt, as she did feel, that it was a question of life and death to her fidelity of purpose and her purity of heart whether she obtained their protection or not. On the whole, we deny altogether that Mr. Hardy has made out his case for Tess. She was pure enough in her instincts, considering the circumstances and the class in which she was born. But she had no deep sense of fidelity to those instincts. If she had, she would not have allowed herself time after time to be turned from the plain path of duty, by the fastidiousness of a personal pride which was quite out of proportion to the extremity of her temptations and her perils. It is no doubt true that her husband behaved with even less fidelity to her than she to him. Perhaps that was natural in such a pagan as Mr. Hardy depicts him. But we cannot for a moment admit that even on his own portraiture of the circumstances of the case, Tess acted as a pure woman should have acted under such a stress of temptation and peril. Though pure in instinct, she was not faithful to her pure instinct. We should, indeed, say that Mr. Hardy, instead of illustrating his conviction that there is no Power who guides and guards those who are faithful to their best lights, has only illustrated what every Christian would admit, that if fine natures will not faithfully adhere to such genuine instincts as they have, they may deteriorate, and will deteriorate, in consequence of that faithlessness

While we cannot at all admire Mr. Hardy's motive in writing this very powerful novel, we must cordially admit that he has seldom or never written anything so truly tragic and so dramatic. The beauty and realism of the delineations of the life on the large dairy-farm; the sweetness and, on the whole, generosity of the various dairymaids' feelings for each other; the vivacity of the description of the cows themselves; the perfect insight into the conditions of rustic lives; the true pathos of Tess's sufferings; the perfect naturalness, and even inevitability, of all her impulses; the strange and horrible mixture of feelings with which she regards her destroyer, when, believing that all her chance of happiness is over, she sells herself ultimately for the benefit of her mother and brother and sisters; the masterful conception of the seducer as a convert to Antinomianism, and the ease with which his new faith gives way to a few recitals by Tess of her husband's ground for scepticism (with which, however, we are not favoured); the brilliant description of the flight of Clare and Tess, and of the curious equanimity with which Tess meets the consciousness of having committed murder, seeing that it has restored her for five days to her husband's heart, —are all pictures of almost unrivalled power, though they evidently proceed from the pantheistic conception that impulse is the law of the universe, and that will, properly so called, is a non-existent fiction. We confess that this is a story which, in spite of its almost unrivalled power, it is very difficult to read, because in almost every page the mind rebels against the steady assumptions of the author, and shrinks from the untrue picture of a universe so blank and godless,—Shelley's 'blank, grey, lampless, deep, unpeopled world.'...   [R. H. HUTTON]

New Review, February 1892

Mr. Hardy's new novel, *Tess of the D'Urbervilles*, demands more space than, in a crowd of hustling books, it is likely to receive. Indeed, the story is an excellent text for a sermon or subtly Spectatorial article on old times and new, on modern misery, on the presence among us of the spirit of Augustus Moddle. That we should be depressed is very natural, all things considered; and, indeed, I suppose we shall be no better till we have got the Revolution over, sunk to the nadir of humanity, and reached the middle barbarism again. Then, *Sursum corda*! Mr. Hardy's story, though probably he does not know it, is a rural tragedy of the last century —reversed. In a little book on *The Quantocks*, by Mr. W. L. Nichols (Sampson Low), may be read the history of 'Poor Jack Walford.' Wordsworth wrote a poem on it in the Spenserian measure, but he felt that his work was a failure, and it remains unpublished. Reverse the *rôles* of the man and woman in this old and true tale, add a good deal of fantastic though not impossible matters about the D'Urbervilles, and you have the elements of *Tess*. The conclusion of *Tess* is rather improbable in this age of halfpenny newspapers and appeals to the British public. The black flag would never have been hoisted, as in the final page. But one is afraid of revealing the story to people who have not yet read it. The persistent melancholy they perhaps like, or perhaps can make up their minds to endure. The rustic heroine, in the very opening of the book, explains to her little brothers that our planet is 'a blighted star.' Her mother possesses 'the mind of a happy child,' yet coolly sends her into conspicuous danger, remarking, 'If he don't marry her afore, he will after.' Poor Tess is set between the lusts of one Alec D'Urberville and the love, such as it was, of one Angel Clare. 'Now Alec was a Bounder,' to quote Mr. Besant; and Angel was a prig, whereas Tess was a human being, of human passions. Here are all the ingredients of the blackest misery, and the misery darkens till 'The President of the Immortals has finished his sport with Tess.' I cannot say how much this phrase jars on one. If there be a God, who can seriously think of Him as a malicious fiend? And if there be none, the expression is meaningless. I have lately been reading the works of an old novelist, who was very active between 1814 and 1831. He is not a terse, nor an accurate, nor a philosophic, nor even a very grammatical writer, but how different, and, to my poor thinking, how much wiser, kinder, happier, and more human is his mood. It is pity, one knows, that causes this bitterness in Mr. Hardy's mood. But Homer is not less pitiful of mortal fortunes and man 'the most forlorn of all creatures that walk on earth,' and Homer's faith cannot be called consolation: yet there is no bitterness in him; and probably bitterness is never a mark of the greatest art and the noblest thought.

There are moral passages of great beauty in *Tess*: for example, in that scene where the bemused villagers stagger home through the moonlight, which casts halos round the shadows of their heads no less than if they had been happy shepherds on the sides of

Latmos. There are exquisite studies of the few remaining idyllic passages in rural life, like that walking of the white-clad women in May, which Mr. Hardy compares to the Cerealia. It certainly does resemble the rite of the Thesmophoria. There are touches highly picturesque and telling, as when the red spot on the ceiling, no bigger than a postage stamp, widens into a broad splash of blood. The style is pellucid, as a rule, but there are exceptions. 'Human mutuality' seems, to myself, an ill phrase. 'There, behind the blue narcotic haze, sat "the tragic mischief" of her drama, he who was to be the blood-red ray in the spectrum of her young life.' Here is an odd mixture of science and literature. A face is, or rather is not, 'furrowed with incarnated memories representing in hieroglyphic the centuries of her family's and England's history.' 'In those early days she had been much loved by others of her own sex and age, and had used to be seen about the village as one of three—all nearly of the same year—walking home from school side by side, Tess being the middle one—in a pink pinafore of a finely reticulated pattern, worn over a stuff frock that had lost its original colour for a nondescript tertiary—marching on upon long, stalky legs, in tight stockings which had little ladder-like holes at the knees, torn by kneeling in the roads and banks in search of vegetable and mineral treasures; her then earth-coloured hair hanging like pot-hooks; the arms of the two outside girls resting round the waist of Tess; her arms on the shoulders of the two supporters.' The question is, does this give the picture intended, or is it a little confusing? Why people who are drinking beer should be said to 'seek vinous bliss' is not apparent. A woman, at the public-house in the evening, finds her troubles 'sinking to minor cerebal phenomena for quiet contemplation, in place of standing as pressing concretions which chafe body and soul.' Here is the very reef on which George Eliot was wrecked. However, tastes differ so much that the blemishes, as they appear to one reader, of Mr. Hardy's works may seem beauty-spots in the eyes of another reader. He does but give us of his best, and if his best be too good for us, or good in the wrong way, if, in short, we are not *en rapport* with him, why, there are plenty of other novelists, alive and dead, and the fault may be on our side, not on his. ANDREW LANG

The Bookman, February 1892

... In Mr. Hardy's case every serious student must have perceived that he has concerned himself deeply with the problems of life, that he has explored the questions of theology and philosophy with an 'anxiety' somewhat foreign to this generation. But 'Tess' is neither a revelation nor a new ethic. It is full of teaching, because it is a book

> 'With subtle penetration entering all
> The myriad corridors of the passionate soul.'

But its first aim is neither to upset nor to establish any system either of theology or ethics. Nor does it seek to deny the reality or the terror or the inevitableness of the transgressor's penalty. It is a faithful presentment of one whom the writer judges to be a pure woman—a woman true to the idea of the sex in his first book, 'a child in pleasure, a woman in pain.' The book is an argument for Tess—an argument steeped in passion, an argument by one who knows that the coarse facts are against him, and who does not try to hide them. He hopes by revealing the soul and the history behind the facts to win the reader's verdict, and his appeal is to humanity in every camp of thought.

We think Mr. Hardy will be much misunderstood if, in this great tragedy, he is taken as dealing primarily with moral problems. He appeals to the most rigid purists, to the most orthodox theologians. The dominant idea of present-day orthodox morality—'the woman pays'—is indeed adopted and enforced. But the history of Tess is the argument which Mr. Hardy addresses to his readers—perhaps half despairingly as far as they are concerned—certainly hoping nothing from the pedant or the Pharisee. For the lax or the prurient there is nothing here. The book is as pure as it is passionate, and however Tess may be judged by those who care to judge her, there can be small doubt that it ranks first among Mr. Hardy's achievements, and second to no work of its time. The end is significant. Tess's unworthy husband and her sister march away from the black flag into a land of promise. She is left dead in the depths of shame, with none to remain with her but her chronicler—whose chief title to honour it will henceforth be that he was the advocate of Tess.

Review of Reviews, February 1892

... If any falling off from Mr. Hardy's best was discernible in 'A Group of Noble Dames,' he has made ample amends in 'Tess of the D'Urbervilles,' which can hardly fail to take rank as its author's greatest work up to the present time. The conception of a girl who, placed in circumstances of extraordinary and overwhelming difficulty, was led, almost irresistibly, to forsake the path of conventional morality, yet retained unimpaired her central virginity of soul, was attended with some dangers, both ethical and artistic, and we do not pretend to think that Mr. Hardy has altogether overcome them. The influence of so-called 'realism,' as understood in France in the latter part of the nineteenth century, is strong both for good and ill in Mr. Hardy's latest work, which in some respects is Zola-esque to a degree likely to alienate not a few well-meaning persons; and in more than one instance we doubt if he has not sacrificed the higher truth of imagination for a narrower and lower kind of fidelity to the ignoble facts of life. . . .

The Academy, 6 February 1892

In this, his greatest work, Mr. Hardy has produced a tragic master-piece which is not flawless, any more than *Lear* or *Macbeth* is; and the easiest way of writing about it would be to concentrate one's attention upon certain blemishes of style, read the author a lecture upon their enormity, affect to be very much shocked and upset by some of his conclusions in morals, and conveniently shirk such minor critical duties as the attempt to abnegate one's prejudices, inherited or acquired; to estimate in what degree the author's undoubtedly impassioned ethical vision is steady and clear; and, while eschewing equally a dogmatic judicialism and a weak sur-render of the right of private censorship, to survey the thing created, in some measure, by the light of its creator's eyes. What is called critical coolness seems, no doubt, on a cursory view, an ex-cellent qualification in a judge of literature; but true criticism, when it approaches the work of the masters, can never be quite cool. To be cool before the *Lear* or the *Macbeth* were simply not to feel *what is there;* and it is the critic's business to feel, just as much as to see. In so tremendous a presence, the criticism which can be cool is no criticism at all. The critical, hardly less than the creative mind, must possess the faculty of being rapt and transported, or its function declines into mere connoisseurship, the pedant's office of mechanical appraisement.

One may, however, feel the greatness of Mr. Hardy's work pro-foundly, and yet be conscious of certain alloying qualities; but let it be said at once, such qualities are of the surface only. None the less, with respect to the over-academic phraseology which here and there crops up in this book. I myself have but one feeling—a wish that it were absent. This terminology of the schools is misplaced; I can feel nothing but regret for these nodosities upon the golden thread of an otherwise fine diction. In a certain sense they disturb a reader all the more for the very reason that they are *not*—like

Mr. Meredith's singularities of speech, for example—ingrained in the very constitution of the style and, obviously, native to the author, nor are they so frequent as to become a habit, a characteristic mannerism which one might get used to; rather they are exceptional and excrescent—foreign to the total character of Mr. Hardy's English—and serve no purpose but to impair the homogeneity of his utterance. The perfect style for a novelist is surely one which never calls attention to its own existence, and there was needed only the omission or modification of a score or two of sentences in these volumes to have assimilated the style of *Tess* to such an ideal. Nothing but gain could have resulted from the elimination of such phrases as 'his former pulsating flexuous domesticity.' Possibly Mr. Hardy intends some self-reference of a defensive sort when he observes that

> 'advanced ideas are really in great part but the latest fashion in definition—a more accurate expression, by words in *logy* and *ism*, of sensations which men and women have vaguely grasped for centuries;'

touching which, one is impelled to ask—Are the words in *logy* and *ism* necessarily more accurate instruments of thought than simpler phrases? Recalling the other memorable case in which a great novelist finally allowed her passion for elaborate precision of statement to metallicise an originally pliant style, one doubts if there was any truer psychological accuracy in the delineation of Deronda than in that of Silas Marner. Mr. Herbert Spencer's diction is no doubt very accurate, but probably not more so than Lord Tennyson's.

Fortunately, however, *Tess* is a work so great that it could almost afford to have even proportionately great faults: and the faults upon which I have dwelt—perhaps unduly—are casual and small. Powerful and strange in design, splendid and terrible in execution, this story brands itself upon the mind as with the touch of incandescent iron. To speak of its gloom as absolutely unrelieved is scarcely correct. Dairyman Crick provides some genuine mirth, though not in too abundant measure; and 'Sir John,' with his 'skellingtons,' is a figure at once humorous and pathetic. But with these exceptions, the atmosphere from first to last is, indeed, tenebrous; and after the initial stroke of doom, Tess appears to us like Thea, in Keats's poem:

> 'There was a listening fear in her regard,
>   As if calamity had but begun,

As if the vanward clouds of evil days
Had spent their malice, and the sullen rear
Was with its stored thunder labouring up.'

The great theme of the book is the incessant penalty paid by the innocent for the wicked, the unsuspicious for the crafty, the child for its fathers; and again and again this spectacle, in its wide diffusion, provokes the novelist to a scarcely suppressed declaration of rebellion against a supramundane ordinance that can decree, or permit, the triumph of such wrong. The book may almost be said to resolve itself into a direct arraignment of the morality of this system of vicarious pain—a morality which, as he bitterly expresses it, 'may be good enough for divinities,' but is 'scorned by average human nature.' Almost at the outset, this note of insurrection against an apparently inequitable scheme of things is struck, if less audaciously, upon our introduction to the Durbeyfield household.

'All these young souls were passengers in the Durbeyfield ship, entirely dependent on the judgment of the two Durbeyfield adults for their pleasures, their necessities, their health, even their existence. If the heads of the Durbeyfield household chose to sail into difficulty, disaster, starvation, disease, degradation, death, thither were these half-dozen little captives under hatches compelled to sail with them—six helpless creatures, who had never been asked if they wished for life on any terms, much less if they wished for it on such hard conditions as were involved in being of the shiftless house of Durbeyfield.'

In one way and another, this implicit protest against what he cannot but conceive to be the maladministration of the laws of existence, this expostulation with 'whatever gods there be' upon the ethics of their rule, is the burden of the whole strain. And a joyless strain it is, whose theme is the havoc wrought by 'those creeds which futilely attempt to check what wisdom would be content to regulate;' the warfare of 'two ardent hearts against one poor little conscience,' wherein the conscience at last is calamitously victorious, the hearts rent and ruined; and, over all, like an enveloping cloud, 'the dust and ashes of things, the cruelty of lust, and the fragility of love.' Truly a stupendous argument; and in virtue of the almost intolerable power with which this argument is wrought out, *Tess* must take its place among the great tragedies, to have read which is to have permanently enlarged the boundaries of one's intellectual and emotional experience.

Perhaps the most subtly drawn, as it is in some ways the most perplexing and difficult character, is that of Angel Clare, with his half-ethereal passion for Tess—'an emotion which could jealously guard the loved one against his very self.' But one of the problems of the book, for the reader, is involved in the question how far Mr. Hardy's own moral sympathies go with Clare in the supreme crisis of his and Tess's fate. Her seducer, the spurious D'Urberville, is entirely detestable, but it often happens that one's fiercest indignation demands a nobler object than such a sorry animal as that; and there are probably many readers who, after Tess's marriage with Clare, her spontaneous disclosure to him of her soiled though guiltless past, and his consequent alienation and cruelty, will be conscious of a worse anger against this intellectual, virtuous, and unfortunate man than they could spare for the heartless and worthless libertine who had wrecked these two lives. It is at this very point, however, that the masterliness of the conception, and its imaginative validity, are most conclusively manifest, for it is here that we perceive Clare's nature to be consistently inconsistent throughout. As his delineator himself says of him: 'With all his attempted independence of judgment, this advanced man was yet the slave to custom and conventionality when surprised back into his early teachings.' He had carefully schooled himself into a democratic aversion from everything connected with the pride of aristocratic lineage; but when he is suddenly made aware that Tess is the daughter of five centuries of knightly D'Urbervilles, he unfeignedly exults in her splendid ancestry. He had become a rationalist in morals no less than an agnostic in religion; yet no sooner does this emancipated man learn from his wife's own most loving lips the story of her sinless fall, than his affection appears to wither at the roots. 'But for the world's opinion,' says Mr. Hardy, somewhat boldly, her experiences 'would have been simply a liberal education.' Yet it is these experiences which place her for a time outside the human sympathy of her husband, with all his fancied superiority to conventionalisms and independence of tradition. The reader pities Clare profoundly, yet cannot but feel a certain contempt for the shallowness of his casuistry, and a keen resentment of his harsh judgment upon the helpless woman—all the more so since it is her own meek and uncomplaining submission that aids him in his cruel punishment of her. 'Her mood of long-suffering made his way easy for him, and she herself was his best advocate.' Considering the proud ancestry whose blood was in her veins, and the high spirit and even fierce temper she exhibits on occasion, one almost wonders at her absolute passivity under such treatment as he subjects her to; but the explanation obviously lies in her own unquestioning conviction of the justice of his procedure. One of Mr. Hardy's especially poetic traits is his manner of sometimes using external Nature not simply as a background or a setting, but as a sort of superior spectator and chorus, that makes strangely unconcerned comments from the vantage-ground of a sublime aloofness upon the ludicrous tragedy of the human lot; and, in the scene of Tess's confession, a singularly imaginative effect is produced by kindred means, where Mr. Hardy makes the very furniture and appurtenances of the room undergo a subtle change of aspect and expression as the bride unfolds her past, and brings Present and Future ruining about her head:

'Tess's voice throughout had hardly risen higher than its opening tone; there had been no exculpatory phrase of any kind, and she had not wept. But the complexion even of external things seemed to suffer transmutation as her announcement progressed. The fire in the grate looked impish—demoniacally funny, as if it did not care in the least about her strait. The fender grinned idly, as if it too did not care. The light from the water-bottle was merely engaged in a chromatic problem. All material objects around announced their irresponsibility with terrible iteration. And yet nothing had changed since the moments when he had been kissing her; or rather, nothing in the substance of things. But the essence of things had changed.'

One detail of this scene strikes me as a crudity in art, though it may be a fact in nature. It is where she is suddenly aghast at the effect of her own confession: 'Terror was upon her white face as she saw it; her cheek was flaccid, *and her mouth had the aspect of a round little hole.*' This may be realism, but even realism is eclectic, and rejects more than it uses; and this is surely one of those non-essential touches which, drawing attention upon themselves, purchase a literal veracity at the expense of a higher imaginative verisimilitude.

After this, D'Urberville's re-intrusion upon her life, and his resumed mastery of it, are matters which, in their curious air of predestination, affect us somewhat in the manner of spectral interferences with human fates; and this impression is incidentally aided by the use made, very sparingly—with that fine, suggestive parsimony which reveals the artist's hand—of the one preternatural detail, the legend of the D'Urberville coach and four. Thenceforward, as the tragedy climbs towards its last summit of desolation and doom, criticism in the ordinary sense must lie low, in the shadow of so great and terrible a conception.

There is one thing which not the dullest reader can fail to recognise—the persistency with which there alternately smoulders and flames through the book Mr. Hardy's passionate protest against the unequal justice meted by society to the man and the woman associated in an identical breach of the moral law. In his wrath, Mr. Hardy seems at times almost to forget that society is scarcely more unjust than nature. He himself proposes no remedy, suggests no escape—his business not being to deal in nostrums of social therapeutics. He is content to make his readers pause, and consider, and pity; and very likely he despairs of any satisfactory solution of the problem which he presents with such disturbing power and clothes with a vesture of such breathing and throbbing life.

WILLIAM WATSON

The Independent, 25 February 1892

Where is the writing of fiction going to? More and more the impulse of genius seems to be away from the contemplation of wholesome, invigorating scenes and toward noisome ones. The two most important works of fiction recently published—most important in point of literary finish and in the power of imagination—the two which will be most read perhaps, and most talked of for some time to come, 'The History of David Grieve' and *Tess of the D'Urbervilles*, are striking examples of this trend.

It is not for us to shut away from the artist the presentation of the dark strains in life and character. Fiction would be one-sided and in the main valueless were it confined to picturing only happy, wholesome folk. Nature is composite, so must art be; and it is as unfair to life to represent it wholly evil as to represent it wholly good. This is true even when we discard every ethical consideration and view art merely as an agent for producing pictures.

What is this fascination which is drawing novelists to adultery as the one most desirable subject? Does the study of human life inevitably lead to regarding illicit intercourse between the sexes as the largest, most important and most interesting fact affecting society? Is everything connected with our advanced state of civilization dominated by the questions arising out of unholy love between man and woman? Shall we quit religion, philosophy, politics, commerce, everything, and turn to a study of adultery?

These are blunt inquiries; but they are pertinent to the issue presented by a novel like *Tess of the D'Urbervilles*.

The story, robbed of clothing, is this: Tess, the heroine, is a poor, beautiful girl. She goes into the house of a wealthy woman, who is blind, to work. The woman's son seduces Tess, altho she does not love him, and she goes back to her lowly home and gives birth to a child which dies. The girl after a time goes to work on a dairy farm where she and a curate's son fall in love with each other. He asks her to marry him; but in memory of her crime she refuses. He insists upon knowing why she cannot marry him; but she will not tell. At length, however, they marry and then he confesses to her that once upon a time he committed adultery or fornication. She forgives him, and feeling that now in response to her magnanimity he will forgive her, tells her story of shame. Up he rises and leaves her, goes off to Brazil nursing his remorse while she nurses hers. Some time after this she goes into a church and sees in the pulpit preaching the man who in the first instance seduced her. He sees her, seeks her out and tries to convert her; but in fact she converts him to infidelity and he quits preaching, falls to cursing and swearing and seduces her again. Then her husband returns full of forgiveness for the old fault only to find her in the midst of the new. So thereupon she murders her seducer and leaps into the arms of her husband. They are not to be happy, however, for the minions of the law take Tess and incarcerate her. The story ends with a lurid tho vague suggestion of an execution, perhaps by hanging; and so Tess is no more.

Thomas Hardy takes his subject and bathes it in the light of his splendid genius. He imagines the situations with absolute dramatic vision, and presents them with startling power. It is incomparably sad and saddening, this story of depravity; for it is a story of depravity despite its sub-title: *A Pure Woman Faithfully Presented.*

Tess was not a pure woman. Pure women do not, save in novels, drop into the arms of men that they do not love. We give our sympathy readily to a girl deceived by a man whom she loves and trusts ignorantly, blindly, under promise of marriage; but even then she is not pure; she is defiled. What he is there is no word vile enough to express.

This whole story is a pretty kettle of fish for pure people to eat, and yet it is not exactly what debauched readers may crave. Mr. Hardy is no Tolstoï, picturing lechery to the last particular, no Zola reveling in filth; he is reserved and clean in the treatment of his subject. You find no gilding and refining of vice, no purple haze or dreamy sheen of glory flung over the ecstasies of debauchery. Still it is possible, it is probable that his method is more dangerous to the moral fiber of young readers than the open French method. The French novelist treats virtue with a sneer; Mr. Hardy offers Tess as the model of a pure woman. In Mr. Hardy's belief we have arrived at a point in civilization where it is not necessary for a girl to lose purity before she becomes the mistress of a man she does not love and does not intend to marry. Even after she has married the man she loves, she may return to the arms of her seducer and still be pure!

We are aware that our review is dealing plainly with a subject not desirable as a dish for conversation in polite circles; but Mr. Hardy's book must be tossed aside unnoticed or be treated sincerely in reviewing it. The value of the work is involved in the view of life it presents; that view is true or it is false. We cannot accept such a story as merely a tale; to do so would be to refuse to notice it. It is sent forth as a presentation of truth through art. Accepting this as the author's aim we do not hesitate to say that he has violated the fundamental purpose of the art of fiction.

The end of all valuable art is to refine and ennoble while it attracts and entertains the human soul. A picture like this of Tess attracts and entertains; but it does not refine and ennoble. The attraction is the force of evil, the entertainment is the fascination of unrelieved misery. Mr. Hardy is a master and in his hands this history of woman's weakness and man's brutality flames with the fire of genius. The artisanship is superb. There is not a living novelist who can approach it in directness, reserve, dramatic energy and rounded perfection of technical skill. But to what good?

Surely Mr. Hardy has not written this story for the delectation of readers! We should be sorry to think that he would pander to the taste of men and women who love to read about girls who fall, and men who make them fall, about preachers who were once seducers of ignorant girls, and who quit preaching to seduce them over again after they are married, about girls who murder their seducers and are hanged therefor! Surely Mr. Hardy does not offer such a mess of pottage as toothsome—as a delicacy for refined palates!

What for, then, is the story written? Ah, reader, let us not push this inquiry too far. Novelists must live, they must attract attention, no matter how. Mr. Hardy knows full well that the story of Tess will not reform men or save women. There will be cases where men will betray and women will pay so long as the world stands, and that long too will both woman and man be defiled by the facts. Mr. Hardy knows and we all know that the writing and reading of novels is not going to keep weak women from forgiving their husbands their sins, or make men forgive their wives their sins. It is a matter of sex, this difference of view; whether it is or not, novels will not change it.

A novel like this story of Tess, then, is nothing after all but a novel. The man reader will light a cigar and open the book to peruse it for pastime; the shop girl will take in a bit of chewing-gum and read with the same object. Who of us feels the need of reading a novel for self-reform? Critics are in the habit of puling in a more or less maudlin spirit over what they call the 'lesson of vice' taught through the 'merciless methods of realism'; but who is it that needs this lesson? Surely not the moralist who reads fiction in cold blood for its moral meaning. Will the poor lass like Tess read Mr. Hardy's novel to her benefit? Will the accomplished *roué* be turned by it to virtue? Mr. Hardy knows the world too well to believe it. Let us not deceive ourselves; we all read novels for pleasure. Evil is fascinating in food, drink, art, literature, life; the novelist knows it and he borrows that fascination for his story; then to ease his conscience he invents a theory which shows that evil is the chief energy of reform and the critics and publishers join him in the profitable venture.

We take it for granted that phases of life like the experiences of Tess will flash out frequently and luridly forever along the trail of time, and we fear that novelists of masterly power will forever write stories like this; but we are 'mercilessly realistic' enough to say straight out that we do not believe that novelists write above all for human reform; they write to sell novels. Nor do we believe that any person reads novels to reform himself—he reads them for pleasure. Reform in either case is an incidental consideration if considered at all.

In this view the story of Tess appeals to human sympathy very strongly and directly; it harrows our hearts, it arouses our anger, it fills us with indignation, and it leaves us depressed and sorrowful. If we are right-minded, and of course we are, what pleasure has this sad story of sin and shame given us? If we are not right-minded what good has it done us? We curl our lips and toss it aside and return to our evil doings. No way out of shame and sin has been shown us, and we already knew the way to death.

As a piece of artisanship this novel is well-nigh perfect; the workman has shown himself a consummate master of his craft; a sense of this superb workmanship is the only pure pleasure the book affords; every other effect is as black as night, as cheerless as a tomb, as hopeless as the scaffold.

Punch, 27 February 1892

In *Tess of the D'Urbervilles* (published by Messrs. OSGOOD, MC-ILVAINE & Co.), Mr. THOMAS HARDY has given us a striking work of fiction, bold in design and elaborate in finish. The characters, with one exception, are as true to life as are his graphic descriptions of nature's own scenery; true that is to the types of such rural life as he professes to represent,—the life led in our Christian country by thousands and thousands of genuine Pagans, superstitious Bœotians, with whom the schoolmaster can do but little, and the parson still less. As to the clergymen who appear in this story, two of them are priggishly academic, a third is a comfortable antiquarian, and the fourth unacquainted with even the A. B. C. of his own pastoral theology.

Since THACKERAY'S *Captain Costigan*, and TOM ROBERTSON'S dramatic variation of him as *Eccles* in *Caste,* no more original type of the besotted, no-working working-man, has been given us ('at least, as far as I am aware,' interpolates the Baron, with a possible reservation) than *Tess's* father, *Durbeyfield*. His foolish wife, *Joan*, kindly in a way, a fair housewife and helpmate, yet deficient in moral sense, is another admirably-drawn character.

The only blot on this otherwise excellent work is the absurdly melodramatic character of that 'villain of the deepest dye,' *Alec D'Urberville,* who would be thoroughly in his element in an Adelphi Drama of the most approved type, ancient or modern. He is just the sort of stage-scoundrel who from time to time seeks to take some mean advantage of a heroine in distress, on which occasions said heroine (of Adelphi Drama) will request him to 'unhand her,' or to 'stand aside and let her pass;' whereupon the dastardly ruffian retaliates with a diabolical sneer of fiendish malice, his eyes ablaze with passion, as, making his melodramatic exit at the O. P. wing, he growls, 'Aha! a day will come!' or 'She must and shall be mine!' or, if not making his exit, but remaining in centre of stage to assist in forming a picture, he exclaims, with fiendish glee, 'Now, pretty one, you are in my power!' and so forth. 'Tis a great pity that such a penny-plain-and-two-pence-coloured scoundrel should have been allowed so strong a part among Mr. HARDY'S excellent and unconventional *dramatis personæ.* Even the very, very strong ejaculations wherein this bold bad man indulges on the slightest provocation belong to the most antiquated vocabulary of theatrical ruffianism. However, there he is, and all the perfumes of the Vale of Blackmoor will not suffice for dispelling the strong odour of the footlights which pervades every scene where this unconscionable scoundrel makes his appearance. That he is ultimately disposed of by being stuck to the heart with the carving-knife that had been brought in for cold-beef slicing at breakfast, is some satisfaction. But far be it from the Baron to give more than this hint in anticipation of the tragic *dénouement*. Some might accuse Mr. THOMAS HARDY of foolhardiness in so boldly telling ugly truths about the Pagan Phyllises and Corydons of our dear old Christian England; but we, his readers, have the author's word for the truth of what he has written, as 'the fortunes of *Tess of the D'Urbervilles, a Pure Woman*,' are 'faithfully presented,' by THOMAS HARDY, and so his honour is pledged to the truth of this story which his powers of narration have made so fascinating to a host of readers besides the one who is a host in himself, namely,

THE BARON DE BOOK-WORMS

Letter from Henry James to Robert Louis Stevenson, 19 March 1892

The good little Thomas Hardy has scored a great success with *Tess of the d'Urbervilles*, which is chock-full of faults and falsity and yet has a singular beauty and charm. . . .

Then, 17 February 1893:

I grant you Hardy with all my heart . . . I am meek and ashamed where the public clatter is deafening—so I bowed my head and let *Tess of the D.'s* pass. But oh yes, dear Louis, she is vile. The pretence of 'sexuality' is only equalled by the absence of it, and the abomination of the language by the author's reputation for style. There are indeed some pretty smells and sights and sounds. But you have better ones in Polynesia.

The Quarterly Review, April 1892
From 'Culture and Anarchy'

. . . We are required to read the story of Tess (or Theresa) Durbeyfield as the story of 'A pure woman faithfully presented by Thomas Hardy.' Compliance with this request entails something of a strain upon the English language. Mr. Squeers once with perfect justice observed that there was no Act of Parliament which could prevent a man from calling his house an island if it pleased him to do so. It is indisputably open to Mr. Hardy to call his heroine a pure woman; but he has no less certainly offered many inducements to his readers to refuse her the name. . . .

. . . Not long since Mr. Hardy published in one of the magazines his recipe for renewing the youth of fiction, which he conceived, and not without justice, to have grown, like Doll Tearsheet, 'sick of a calm.' The national taste and the national genius have returned, he said, to the great tragic motives so greatly handled by the drama-tists of the Periclean and Elizabethan ages. But the national genius perceives also that these tragic motives 'Demand enrichment by further truths—in other words, original treatment; treatment which seeks to show Nature's unconsciousness, not of essential laws, but those laws framed merely as social expedients by humanity, without a basis in the heart of things.' Here, it will be observed, Mr. Hardy speaks only, and prudently, for himself as representing the national genius, being evidently conscious that the national taste might decline his interpretation. But was there ever such foolish talking? Mr. Hardy must have read the dramatists of the Periclean and Elizabethan ages very carelessly, or have strangely forgotten them, if he conceives that there is any analogy between their great handling of great tragic motives and this clumsy sordid tale of boorish brutality and lust. Has the common feeling of humanity against seduction, adultery, and murder no basis in the heart of things? It is the very foundation of human society. In the explanatory note from which we have already quoted, a sentence of St. Jerome's is offered as a sop to 'Any too genteel reader who cannot endure to have it said what everybody thinks and feels.' Does everybody then think and feel that seduc-tion, adultery, and murder have their basis in the heart of things, that they are the essential laws of Nature? If Mr. Hardy's apology means anything at all, it can mean only that. His apology is, in truth, as much beside the mark as the sentence from St. Jerome with which he thinks to enforce it: 'If an offence come out of the truth, better is it that the offence come than that the truth be con-cealed.' Now this,—and here we must be excused for plain speaking —this is pure cant, and that worst form of cant which takes its stand on a mischievous reading of the old aphorism, 'To the pure all things are pure.' St. Jerome's argument would be a good one enough to salve the conscience of a delicate-minded witness in a court of law, who in the interests of truth might be required to speak of inconvenient things. It is absolutely no argument for a novelist who, in his own interests, has gratuitously chosen to tell a coarse and disagreeable story in a coarse and disagreeable manner.

As we have found fault with Mr. Hardy's manner, equally with his subject, we must spare a few words to that. Coarse it is not, in the sense of employing coarse words; indeed he is too apt to affect a certain preciosity of phrase which has a somewhat incongruous effect in a tale of rustic life; he is too fond,—and the practice has been growing on him through all his later books—of writing like a man 'who has been at a great feast of languages and stolen the scraps,' or, in plain English, of making experiments in a form of language which he does not seem clearly to understand, and in a style for which he was assuredly not born. It is a pity, for Mr. Hardy had a very good style of his own once, and one moreover excellently suited to the subjects he knew and was then content to deal with. The coarseness and disagreeableness of his present manner come from within rather than from without. That they come unconsciously we most willingly believe; indeed it would be only charity to suppose that they come from an inherent failure in the instinct for good taste, and a lack of the intellectual cultivation that can sometimes avail to supply its place, added to a choice of subject which must always be fatal to an author, no matter what his other gifts may be, who has not those two safeguards. But whatever be their origin, there they are and must be apparent to the simplest reader. To borrow a familiar phrase, Mr. Hardy never fails to put the dots on all his i's, he never leaves you in doubt as to his meaning. Poor Tess's sensual qualifications for the part of heroine are paraded over and over again with a persistence like that of a horse-dealer egging on some wavering customer to a deal, or a slave-dealer appraising his wares to some full-blooded pasha. . . .

MOWBRAY MORRIS

The Fortnightly Review, 1 July 1892

. . . The central conception of the book, the main feature, seems right enough, but it has not been seized strongly, and the story, like all Mr. Hardy's stories, alternately hurries or flags. Parts are good enough as renderings of human and natural life to make one more than astonished at the not unfrequent lapses into the cheapest conventional style of the average popular novelist. . . .

To say nothing of the improbability of four milkmaids, all sleeping in one room, and all hopelessly in love with one blameless prig of an amateur gentleman farmer, what a shocking want of the sense of both humour and variety does he show in creating such a situation! It is scarcely to be wondered at that these imaginary dairy-maids soon begin to talk as never dairy-maids talked on this earth. . . .

The same weakness drives Mr. Hardy to mar the evanescent reality of Tess herself. He will make her talk sometimes as the author of *Far from the Madding Crowd* is often wont to write. Her lover presses upon her a course of study in history; but she refuses.

'Because what's the use of learning that I am one of a long row

only—finding out that there is set down in some old book some-
body just like me, and to know that I shall only act her part;
making me sad, that's all. The best is not to remember that your
nature and your past doings have been just like thousands and
thousands, and that your coming life and doings'll be like thousands and thousands. . . . I shouldn't mind learning why the sun
shines on the just and the unjust alike, but that is what books
will not tell me.'

Tess, it is true, as Mr. Hardy continually remarks, had passed her
Sixth Standard; but even agricultural girls of the Sixth Standard
are scarcely yet credible with a 'criticism of life' of this calibre. It
is terrible to see a storyteller so unaware of what constitutes the
one possible charm of his chief figure. Imagine Goethe making
Marguerite talk like that! And it is not that Mr. Hardy is not at
times able to render character. D'Urberville, for instance, in the
first two parts is recognizably drawn from the life; but that does
not prevent a shadowy masquerade of this vicious brute appearing
for a short period later on as a ranting preacher. It is not that
vicious brutes may not become ranting preachers. They may, and
do; but that this particular vicious brute of Mr. Hardy's, thanks to
the want of energy in his realization, does nothing of the kind.

One artistic gift Mr. Hardy has which rarely seems to desert him,
and that is what Henri Beyle calls so aptly *l'originalité de lieu*. His
people are at one with his places, a single harmonious growth of
spiritual and natural circumstance, and this, the true artistic
charity, covers, or helps to cover, a multitude of sins. The best
examples of it reach high, indeed as high as anything of the kind
now done among us. What else but this renders credible and even
poignantly real the final wanderings of the two lovers world-weary
and doomed. [The murder, of course, is absurd.] The love-nest
in the empty furnished home of strangers, an incident super-
ficially so improbable, is only less actual than the weird journey to
Stonehenge, and Tess's sacrificial sleep on the altar-stone. After all,
the book has in it the sob of the earth's suffering, 'the sense of
tears in mortal things,' the vain struggle of the human heart against
unjust fatality; and of how many books, not to say of how many
novels, that appear in this England in a generation can one say so
much?—in this England where the novel has become the helpless
prey of the Philistine and Philistiness—where the only variety
possible on the banalities of an ignorant and abject conventionality
seems to be fantastic revels in the English tongue, and the literary
woe and abomination alluded to by more than one of the prophets.

Yet one cannot for a moment hesitate in one's recognition of the fact that Mr. Hardy's novel is not a success—is a failure. It is far too faulty to pass. The gaps that represent bad work are too large and too frequent. One has no desire to come back to it. A second reading leaves a lower estimate of it than the first, and a third is not possible. There is the immense pity of it. The artistic blemishes which were in Mr. Hardy's early books might, and in all probability would, have been eradicated if from the beginning he had had to face anything like genuine criticism, anything like a genuinely critical public. But, as it was, he was praised for his bad work and blamed for his good, until the faculty of distinction in him became hopelessly blurred and bewildered. The grotesque worthlessness of the criticism which he, like all the rest of us, received and receives in the ravenous and whirling columns of the press, he must soon have learned to rate at its true value for a serious writer. But the critical effort (and that comes to mean the effort in what may be called comparative culture) which still alone can prove the salvation of such an one among ourselves, this he does not seem to have made. The result is that his most ambitious work, which should have proved a masterpiece and which contains the elements of a masterpiece, has absolutely missed its aim and falls away. 'This sort cometh not out save by prayer and fasting.'. . .

FRANCIS ADAMS

Review of Reviews, July 1892
A Woman's View of Tess

Harriet Waters Preston, writing on Thomas Hardy in the *Century Magazine*, gives a woman's view of 'Tess of the D'Urbervilles' with considerable emphasis. After describing how Tess, after her first misfortune, was borne safely and almost triumphantly through all her dangers, she says:—

'The goal is close at hand where, in Mr. Hardy's own striking words concerning the Native, the fairest child of his fancy may grasp the supreme boon of *retreating from life without shame*. We are actually beginning to thank him for an enlarged perception of the moral possibilities of primitive womanhood. The interest of the narrative has been breathless all along; now, at its final crisis, our pulses begin to throb as though we were on the eve of some stupendous revelation. Has our pantheist and pessimist of other days, we ask, been transformed into the most powerful and penetrating of all the preachers of Neo-Christianity? Are we about to be told, at last, what the words were which Jesus 'stooped down and with his finger wrote on the ground, as though he heard them not'—the mystic import of the divine sentence, 'Neither do I condemn thee: go, and sin no more'?

'Alas! nothing of the sort. Mr. Hardy's conversion is no more authentic than Alec D'Urberville's own. Just when his noble work lacks naught but the finishing touch, he is seized by what looks like a paroxysm of blind rage against his own creation, and with one violent blow he destroys irreparably both its symmetry and its significance. There was no need to condemn the finest of his creations to an after-life of bourgeois security and prosperity as the wife of Angel Clare. That would have been at once too bad for her and too good for him. But surely a kindly, compassionate, natural death might have rescued Tess from her sharp dilemma at any one of the later turnings of her hunted way! Or, if not, she had still the last remedy in her own hand, and the daughter of the D'Urbervilles would never have lacked the courage to apply it. But from the moment when, despite the dreadful illumination of her experience, and the painfully acquired habit of heroic resistance, Tess yields a second time to the importunities of her first and now doubly repulsive seducer, the claim put forth for her by her historian upon his title-page is stultified; and artistically, no less than morally, his work lies in ruin. To call Tess 'pure' after this is a ferocious sarcasm. The first stain had been effaced by a purgatory of suffering; the second is indelible. The ghastly incidents crowded into the last pages of the book avail nothing. The murder and the scaffold are mere vulgar horrors, gratuitously insulting to the already outraged feelings of the deeply disappointed reader. They exceed the proper limit of tragedy, exciting neither 'pity' nor 'terror,' but simply repugnance. No writer of our own gloomy time—I say it regretfully, and even resentfully—has grasped for one moment, only to wantonly fling away, a more sublime opportunity than Mr. Hardy in 'Tess of the D'Urbervilles.'

Black and White, 27 August 1892
A Chat with the Author of 'Tess'

It will be perhaps the simplest and most interesting procedure on my part that I should tell my readers something about Mr. Thomas Hardy, himself and his surroundings, before going into the weightier matters of the law into which we were compelled in our discussion upon his last production, 'Tess of the D'Urbervilles; a Pure Woman Faithfully Presented.' Mr. Hardy is in himself a gentle and a singularly pleasing personality. Of middle height, with a very thoughtful face and rather melancholy eyes, he is nevertheless an interesting and amusing companion. He is regarded by the public at large as a hermit ever brooding in the far-off seclusion of a west country village. A fond delusion, which is disproved by the fact that he is almost more frequently to be seen in a London drawing-room, or a Continental hotel, than in the quiet old-world lanes of rural Dorsetshire. His wife, some few years younger than himself, is so particularly bright, so thoroughly *au courant du jour*, so evidently a citizen of the wide world, that the, at first, unmistakable reminiscence that there is in her of Anglican ecclesiasticism is curiously puzzling and inexplicable to the stranger, until the information is vouchsafed that she is intimately and closely connected with what the late Lord Shaftesbury would term 'the higher order of the clergy.'

Nor are their surroundings less interesting than themselves. The house is built on ground within a mile of Dorchester, which was given by Edward III. to his son the Black Prince; it was purchased some years ago of the Duchy of Cornwall by Mr. Thomas Hardy, who I may mention is a magistrate, and who thus becomes the first freeholder of other than Royal blood for many hundreds of years. Beneath the building itself have been discovered the skeletons and the relics of those Romans who, fifteen hundred years ago, were encamped here in great force, and remains of whose Latinity are still to be discerned in the dialect and features of some of the interesting and complex rusticities by whom Mr. Hardy is surrounded, and of whom he is so fond of writing. Pieces of red Samian, rare specimens of ancient pottery, fragments of iridescent glass, most of them discovered on his own ground by Mr. Hardy himself, meet the eye at every turn. Upon the walls hang the original illustrations of his different stories, which have been given him by his friends, Professor Herkomer, Mr. Alfred Parsons and others, whilst Mrs. Hardy's clever little water-colours go far to prove the verisimilitude of her husband's delightful fictions. In the dining-room, and overlooking the sunny breakfast table, the painting of Mr. Hardy himself—looking, with his full beard, strangely unlike the almost clean-shaven person with whom I am talking—confronts the little engraved portrait of Admiral Sir Thomas Hardy—who was, I presume, a relative of the novelist—and in whose arms Lord Nelson passed away in the hour of his greatest triumph.

It was by the drawing-room fire that we sat discussing the frail but charming 'Tess.'

'You cannot imagine how many letters my husband received,'

said Mrs. Hardy, 'begging him to end his story brightly. One dear old gentleman of over eighty wrote, absolutely insisting upon her complete forgiveness and restitution.' 'And why did you not, Mr. Hardy?' said I. 'Surely without any very great stretching of points Tess might have left with Angel when he returned to her, and so have avoided her last great sin, with its fearful punishment?'

Mr. Hardy shook his head.

'No,' he replied, 'the optimistic "living happy ever after" always raises in me a greater horror by its ghastly unreality than the honest sadness that comes of a logical and inevitable tragedy.

'The murder that Tess commits is the hereditary quality, to which I more than once allude, working out in this impoverished descendant of a once noble family. That is logical. And again, it is but a simple transcription of the obvious that she should make reparation by death for her sin. Many women who have written to me have forgiven Tess because she expiated her offence on the scaffold. You ask why Tess should not have gone off with Clare, and "lived happily ever after." Do you not see that under *any* circumstances they were doomed to unhappiness? A sensitive man like Angel Clare could never have been happy with her. After the first few months he would inevitably have thrown her failings in her face. He did not recoil from her after the murder it is true. He was in love with her failings then I suppose; he had not seen her for a long time; with the inconsistency of human nature he forgave the greater sin when he could not pardon the lesser, feeling perhaps that by her desperate act she had made some reparation. She had done what she could. She had done exactly what I think one of her nature under similar circumstances would have done in real life. It is led up to right through the story. One looks for the climax. One is not to be cheated out of it by the exigencies of inartistic conventionality. And so there come the tears of faithful tragedy in place of the ghastly and affected smile of the conventionally optimistic writer. And it is the very favourable reception by the public of this sad ending to my story that has impressed me as a good sign. At one time a publisher would tell you that "a tragic ending" was always a failure. Now, however, people have studied more fully the fictions of all time, and are infinitely more artistic.'

At this moment Mrs. Hardy placed in my hand a sketch by Mr. H. J. Moule, which sketch, drawn on the spot, represents the actual house in which the bride's confession—the turning point of the whole story—took place. "That is Woolbridge Manor House,' explained my host, 'one of the seats of the ———, the family to whom Tess belonged by right of her descent. In that house and on that same night, if you remember, she tried on the jewels that Clare gave her. I think I must tell you that that was an idea of Mrs. Hardy's.' 'And a very pretty and effective idea it was,' I replied, with which opinion my feminine readers are sure to agree. 'And, Mr. Hardy,' I went on, 'it is no mere figment of your brain that Tess was of ancient lineage, and possessed of more old "skelingtons" than anyone else in the country.'

'Oh, no,' replied the author. 'It is an absolute fact. I will go and fetch you the genealogical tree of the actual family.' While he was out of the room Mrs. Hardy told me of her overhearing some labourer boasting to a friend of the vault at Bere Regis, which was full of the 'skelingtons' of his family. It was a fact, she said, that this man was always addressed by an antiquarian clergyman as 'Sir John'; 'for,' said he, 'he *is* Sir John.' And she was much interested, as was Mr. Hardy, when I told them that on a very recent occasion, in an old Northamptonshire church, I had stood by the carved effigy of a crusader, whose embalmed heart, brought home from the land of the Saracens, was visible in an adjacent pillar; and that the only living descendant of the family was an old labourer who lived in the village, where his long dead ancestors had once reigned supreme.

'Exactly,' replied Mr. Hardy, 'there are many such cases about here. You will trace noble lineage in many a face, and there is a certain conscious pride about some of these people which differentiates them at once from middle class cockneyism or provincialism. And in another sense, the rather free and easy mode of life adopted by the squires of the last century, has contributed to the ancient lineage and to the fine features of many of the labouring classes in this neighbourhood. A gentleman told me the other day of a whole village to which he was related through his grandfather. Here is the pedigree of Tess's family,' said my host, as he placed an enormous volume in my hand. And here I traced, without a break, right back to the Conquest, the records of this stately house. 'Woolbridge Manor House,' continued Mr. Hardy after a time, 'as you can see by Mr. Moule's sketch, is only a farmhouse now. The farmer's wife has lately been much exercised as to what the many pilgrimages to her house have meant. You will see on the stairs, exactly as I have described, those two dreadful portraits of Tess's ancestresses; and only a few weeks ago a number of records of the family were discovered hidden away amongst the rafters in the roof.'

'I suppose, Mr. Hardy, that most of your characters are drawn from life?' 'Oh yes, almost all of them. Tess, I only once saw in the flesh. I was walking along one evening and a cart came along in which was seated my beautiful heroine, who, I must confess, was urging her steed along with rather unnecessary vehemence of language. She coloured up very much when she saw me, but—as a novelist—I fell in love with her at once and adopted her as my heroine. Old Mr. Clare was a Dorsetshire parson whose name still lives enshrined in the hearts of thousands. "Shepherd Oak," in "Far from the Madding Crowd," I knew well as a boy; while "Bathsheba Everdene" is a reminiscence of one of my own aunts. Our family, you know, has lived here for centuries. ''Joseph Poorgrass,'' "Eustacia," and "Susan Nonsuch'' in the "Return of the Native," were all well-known local characters. Girls resembling the three dairymaids in "Tess" used to get me to write their love-letters for them when I was a little boy. I suppose,' he went on, replying to a question, 'that unconsciously I absorbed a good deal of their mode of life and speech, and so I have been able to reproduce it in the dairy at "Talbothays".'

I observed how thoroughly and effectually he had disposed of the current conception of Hodge as a mere soulless, mindless humanity. Replied Mr. Hardy, 'And what a ridiculous idea! The English peasantry as a rule are full of character and sentiment which are less often found in the strained, calculating, unromantic middle classes. As I have said in "Tess," so I say now, "Hodge" is a delusion. Rustic ideas, the modes, the surroundings, appear retrogressive and unmeaning at first. After a time, if you live amongst them, you will find as Angel Clare found, that variety takes the place of monotony. The people begin to differentiate themselves, as in a chemical process. The labourer is disintegrated into a number of varied fellow creatures, beings of many minds, infinite in difference: some happy, many serene, a few depressed, one here and there, bright even to genius; some stupid, others wanton, others austere; some mute Miltons, some potential Cromwells. The men strong, heroic souls; the girls dainty heroines. Much of which I ascribe to the fact that in many cases our peasantry is the sole remnant of mediæval England.'

On the following morning, frosty and brilliant, Mr. Hardy took me for a stroll, pointing out as we walked along 'Egdon Heath,' which, bathed in sunshine, lay in the far blue distance. 'Between the heath and us, in that hollow there,' said he, 'is Talbothay's dairy. The road running whitely through the moorland leads to the "Trumpet Major's" home near Weymouth. And here,' said he, a few minutes later, as he pointed to an old red-brick house standing on the outskirts of Dorchester, which of course is known to all Mr. Hardy's readers as 'Casterbridge,' 'here is where Judge Jeffries lodged in the Bloody Assize, and upon the spot on which we are now standing, and which to this day is called "Gallows Hill," he one morning hanged eighty people.'

Turning away from the town we presently found ourselves pacing up and down the old Roman amphitheatre, where once had been realised the wild beast's spring, the victim's shriek, the plaudits of the cruel thousands; where long after—in 1705—a hundred thousand people had gathered to watch the burning alive of some poor wretch who had poisoned her husband. All was still now, and as peaceful and sunny as on that day when 'the Mayor of Casterbridge' met his wife at the old Roman encampment. In the distance rising against the sky, Maiden Castle, with its Titanic personality, compelled the senses to regard it and consider. Here, far from the madding crowd, uninfluenced by modern conventionalism, unrestrained by Mrs. Grundy, Mr. Hardy and I, pacing up and down the green yielding grass, very seriously discussed the moral aspects afforded to the thoughtful reader by his extraordinary and really magnificent presentment of *Tess of the D'Urbervilles*.

'But now Mr. Hardy,' said I, 'I have to quarrel with you for your deliberate description of "Tess" as a *pure* woman. For the moment please you will regard me as a representative of the British public, of the narrow-minded as of the liberal, of the club man in Piccadilly as of Mrs. Grundy in some provincial town. You must let me state the case. I can quite understand that you claim a purity for poor Tess after her *first* fall, the outcome, as she pitifully tells her mother, of sheer ignorance. But how on earth you can describe her as a pure woman after her absolutely unnecessary return to Alec D'Urberville, I cannot conceive; for you cannot plead with F. W. Robertson, of Brighton, that in her case "a woman's worst fault arises from a perverted idea of self-sacrifice." And to add to her sin a cruel murder is, at first sight, absolutely unjustifiable.'

'Very well,' replied Mr. Hardy, 'but I still maintain that her innate purity remained intact to the very last; though I frankly own that a certain outward purity left her on her last fall. I regarded her then as being in the hands of circumstances, not morally responsible, a mere corpse drifting with the current to her end.' 'And then again,' said I, 'you appear to ignore the idea much put forward of late by certain very earnest people that purity is as binding on men as on women, when you depict that very odious young gentleman, Angel Clare, casting off his wife for an offence of ignorance, and yet the very next week proposing to elope with her friend. I grant you that you are true to human nature. Sometimes it seems impossible for the most high-minded reformers to attempt to legislate for us *men*, as though we were angels. They doubtless are theoretically right, but practically they are hopelessly in the wrong. Nature herself is against them. Remorselessly she exacts a purity in woman which she does not demand from man; and you have shown this truth in "Tess" I think.'

Mr. Hardy replied: 'Exactly. That is what I have striven to show. I have adhered to *human nature*. I draw no inferences, I don't even feel them. I only try to give an artistic shape to standing facts. Angel Clare you describe as odious. Well, I have had many letters from men who say they would have done exactly as he did. Angel is a type of a certain class of the modern young man. Cruel, but not intentionally so. It was the fault of his fastidious temperament. Had he not been a man of great subtilty of mind, he would have followed his brothers into the church. But he had intellectual freedom in the dairy. A subtle, poetical man, he preferred that life to the conventional life.'

'Yes,' I replied with a smile, 'and a number of pretty dairymaids to fall in love with him.'

'Ah,' interpolated Mr. Hardy, 'all my men correspondents condemn that as impossible; all my women friends say it is exactly what would have happened.' With which I quite agreed. 'For them, poor dears,' said I, 'a gentleman would exercise an irresistible fascination. But, Mr. Hardy,' I continued, 'why boast of his freedom from convention when, at the most crucial moment, he shows himself as much a slave to it all as his very priggish brothers would have been?'

'Precisely, that is the inconsistency of human nature,' replied Mr. Hardy; 'he always professed to despise ancient lineage, and yet as a matter of fact he was delighted that Tess was a D'Urberville.'

'I revel,' said I, 'in your delineations of feminine character, Mr. Hardy. I fancy you realise with me the fact that, in the case of women especially, *les extrêmes se touchent*. Human nature is far stronger in the Duchess and the dairymaid than it is in the daughter of the lawyer or the draper at Little Pedlington. You would find far more "Tesses" amongst the aristocracy then you would amongst middle-class provincials.'

'That is probably true,' was the reply. 'One often notices in the woman of position the same transparency of passions, the same impulses, the same gentle, candid femininity that you meet with in dairymaids. The higher or the lower you go, the more natural are the people—especially the women. Hence, perhaps, they are deceived more easily.'

'Yes,' I answered, 'they greatly loving, greatly dare.' I pursued the train of thought and asked Mr. Hardy if he had discovered—as I myself on a recent occasion had found out—that Mrs. Grundy has different faces, and that in consequence protestations and approvals came from the most unexpected quarters. 'Certainly I have,' replied he. 'Every clergyman I know has broadly approved of my book as a story, and especially of the christening scene, which, in deference to the advice of a certain friend of mine, a thorough man of the world, I had left out in the serial publication of "Tess".'

'You must have felt it a pain to bring her to so fearful and end.'

'Yes,' said Mr. Hardy, 'such dreams are we made of that I often think of the day when, having decided that she must die, I went purposely to Stonehenge to study the spot. It was a very gloomy, lowering day, and the skies almost seemed to touch the pillars o the great heathen temple.'

'And the ultimate result of your book, Mr. Hardy, will be, I hope, that a greater freedom will exist for the decent, grave consideration of certain deep problems of human life.'

'Well,' replied Mr. Hardy with a smile, 'that would be a very ambitious hope on my part. Remember I am only a learner in the art of novel writing. Still I do feel very strongly that the position of man and woman in nature, things which everyone is thinking and nobody saying, may be taken up and treated frankly. Until lately novelists have been obliged to arrange situations and *dénouements* which they knew to be indescribably unreal, but dear to the heart of the amiable library subscriber. See how this ties the hands of a writer who is forced to make his characters act unnaturally, in order that he may produce the spurious effect of their being in harmony with social forms and ordinances.'

RAYMOND BLATHWAYT

The Quarterly Review, April 1904
From *The Novels of Thomas Hardy*

. . . By way of contrast the story is lightened with a series of beautiful pictures representing the varied business of farming in Wessex at a period when the continuity with the past remained in all things unbroken.

'Between the mother, with her fast-perishing lumber of superstitions, folk-lore, dialect, and orally transmitted ballads, and the daughter, with her trained National teachings and Standard knowledge under an infinitely Revised Code, there was a gap of two hundred years as ordinarily understood. When they were together the Jacobean and the Victorian ages were juxtaposed.'

The difference between Joan Durbeyfield and her child Tess represents the difference in social atmosphere between 'Far from the Madding Crowd' and 'Tess of the D'Urbervilles.' There are other works of Mr Hardy, equally fine, but upon the excellences of which we cannot, in this brief estimate, enlarge, such as 'The Trumpet-Major,' 'The Mayor of Casterbridge,' and the 'Wessex Tales,' in which the same conditions prevail as in 'Far from the Madding Crowd.' They are pictures of rustic life prior to 1851, when newspapers and modern thought, railways and industrialism began to effect in the minds and the mode of living of the peasantry a change, hastened by the result of the Education Act of 1870.

Mr Hardy seems to be divided in opinion with regard to the alteration. The poet and lover of nature contend in him with the equalitarian. The fruits of even legitimate ambition have been purchased at the price of contentment and simple pleasures. In gaining by agitation better wages and a position of greater independence, the peasants have forfeited something more than picturesqueness of appearance. In 'Far from the Madding Crowd' the memorable Joseph Poorgrass and his companions had certain intimate and kindly relations with the land upon which they laboured, not possessed by their less dependent successors. Living and dying on the spot where their forefathers had lived and died, they lost the character of hirelings in that of natural guardians; and, although none of them would have been so terribly bold as the new man, Andrew Candle, who lost a place by telling the squire that his soul was his own, they acquired, by way of compensation, that sympathy with their surroundings, that sense of long local participation, which are not least among the pleasures of life. . . .

EDWARD WRIGHT

❲ *Tess*, as these selections make clear, had a mixed reception. Many of the reviewers acclaimed it as Hardy's masterpiece; others rebuked it for improbability, for realism, for immodesty, above all for immorality. The charge of immodesty must seem merely quaint to us today. By modern standards, Hardy seems scarcely less reticent than other Victorians, but here we find him attacked by the

Saturday Review because he 'leaves little unsaid' and includes such disagreeable details as a mention of Tess's 'fulness of growth, which made her appear more of a woman than she really was'. We shall see this same quaintness, exaggerated into something more serious and dangerous, in the case of *Jude*.

Most of those who attacked *Tess* did so not for its immodesty but for its immorality; the critic of *The Independent*, who was one of the most furious of all, even conceded that 'Mr. Hardy is no Tolstoï, picturing lechery to the last particular, no Zola reveling in filth; he is reserved and clean in the treatment of his subject.' The quaintness seems to have shifted to Tolstoï here; but this critic, though he may have nodded—or snorted—over *Anna Karenina*, did at least read *Tess* with some attention. The battle whether *Tess* is a wicked book rages all through these reviews. *The Independent*, clearly proud of its bluntness, refuses to consider Tess a pure woman: 'Pure women do not, save in novels, drop into the arms of men that they do not love.' The epigraph, 'A Pure Woman', which Hardy so misguidedly added to his title page, in fact caused more indignation than anything else. *The Critic* (not here included), an American paper, complained that this epigraph makes it harder, not easier, to sympathise with Tess: fearing that we are being got at, we resist the author's protestations. Hutton, in *The Spectator*, is more temperate in tone than most, but makes a similar point: 'Though pure in instinct she was not faithful to her pure instinct.' All these critics—as well as others not here included—attack the book from a moral standpoint.

Perhaps this dates them: it is harder nowadays to think of Hardy as undermining morality. And so the defenders of the book (*The Daily Chronicle*, William Watson in *The Academy*) may seem dated too, for they are just as moral. Watson sees indignation where *The Daily Chronicle* sees simple pessimism, but they agree that tragedy is important because it teaches.

As it happens, we have Hardy's own defence, as well as that of his critics. The interview by Raymond Blathwayt in *Black and White* is a particularly interesting document: it must be one of the earliest literary interviews, and there is no way of knowing how reliable it is. Some parts seem to have the ring of fidelity; some parts are confirmed by what we learn from F. E. Hardy's *Life*. The passages immediately relevant to this question are the two discussions of *Tess*: that beginning in the third paragraph ('It was by the drawing-room fire . . .'), and the last third or so of the article ('But now Mr. Hardy . . .') The keystone of his argument is the following:

> 'Very well,' replied Mr. Hardy, 'but I still maintain that her innate purity remained intact to the very last; though I frankly own that a certain outward purity left her on her last fall.'

This is similar to *The Speaker*'s claim that Hardy set out to show problems of conduct to us 'in a new aspect', to see Tess 'with larger, other eyes than ours'. It is natural to ask how convincing this defence is: *what* does Hardy see with his other eyes? The moralising of these critics may make them remote from us: does that mean the battle about Tess is over, or can we find anything in the novel that worries us, on our terms, and to which these solemn reviewers were trying to point? This question is discussed at length by Laurence Lerner in *The Truthtellers* (Part I § 15: '*Tess of the D'Urbervilles*: a Behaviourist Complaint').

Hardy's *Preface* to the fifth edition of the novel is widely available: but perhaps it is nonetheless worth quoting here two sentences from it—those in which he complains of the objectors who

> 'reveal an inability to associate the idea of the sub-title adjective with any but the artificial and derivative meaning which has resulted to it from the ordinances of civilization. They ignore the meaning of the word in Nature, together with all aesthetic claims upon it, not to mention the spiritual interpretation afforded by the finest side of their own Christianity.'

The rest of Blathwayt's interview has a different interest, and seems reliable. The anecdote of the genealogical tree confirms the impression made by the novel itself: the decline of the D'Urbervilles into Durbeyfields is clearly meant to be the sort of thing that really happens. Indeed, it is even possible that the genealogical tree which Hardy fetched was his own—either that of the Hardys, who had come over from Jersey in the fifteenth century, and retained their links with the island, and who included an Elizabethan Thomas Hardy, benefactor of Dorchester Grammar School, as well as Captain Thomas Hardy, captain of the *Victory* at Trafalgar; or else that of the Childs, from whom he was descended on his mother's side, and who believed themselves to have come down in the world.

Besides the question of its immorality, there are two main lines
that criticism of *Tess* can follow: to see it as tragedy, a working-
out of fate, a version of the human condition; or to see it as social
analysis, a study of change in nineteenth-century England. A really
fine critic will link the two, but there tends to be an emphasis one
way or another.

It was the first group of critics who praised *Tess* most: those who
saw it as a tragic masterpiece, an account of woman's lot, with the
power of a Greek drama. Two objections qualify this praise: that
Hardy is too gloomy, and that he invokes Fate too easily, twisting
his plot against the heroine with cruel glee. The first objection now
has, perhaps, a touch of the same quaintness as the charge of
immodesty: neither Hardy nor George Eliot (of whom the same
was said) can seem to us all that gloomy, in the light of what has
been written since. The second objection is still held: Hardy *does*
twist his plots, he does hound Tess with cruel mischance. Andrew
Lang speaks for many critics: 'If there be a God, who can seriously
think of him as a malicious fiend? And if there be none, the expression ("The President of the Immortals had finished his
sport . . .") is meaningless.' This is very much the same objection
as William Empson's, though the vocabulary—and the attitude—
has changed:

> 'To believe in a spirit who only jeers at you is superstitious with-
> out having any of the advantages of superstition; besides, it has
> a sort of petty wilfulness, it comes of trying to think of something
> nasty to say.'   *The Structure of Complex Words*

Some critics praised the book as a tragedy, but deplored it morally:
Hutton in *The Spectator* is the clearest example. This is not surprising in 1892, and perhaps it is not surprising to find something
like the opposite in the twentieth century. D. H. Lawrence, in his
fascinating and almost lunatic *Study of Thomas Hardy*, has what
amounts to a moral criticism of the book. Hardy, he complains, is
unjust to Alec, the physical Alec, the 'rare man'—that same Alec
whom Andrew Lang called a bounder, and whom others did not
consider worthy of a novel.

Consideration of Hardy as a social critic has grown quite common today: two of the best examples are Arnold Kettle (in his
Introduction to the English Novel) and Raymond Williams (in

Critical Quarterly for Winter 1964). In 1892 this approach was much less common, and what there was of it was largely unfavourable. Thus Francis Adams, in the *Fortnightly*, finds Tess speaking beyond the range of her social origins: 'Even agricultural girls of the Sixth Standard are scarcely yet credible with a "criticism of life" of this calibre.' Raymond Williams, as it happens, addresses himself to this very point, and his article is a defence of Hardy as a social observer who was shrewd and, in a complex fashion, involved. It is a view that Hardy took of himself, as his prefaces make clear. He would have been pleased, surely, with what *The Speaker* said in its opening paragraph, as he might well have been pleased with Mr. Williams's article. Here again the Blathwayt interview is revealing.

8 · JUDE THE OBSCURE

❬ Hardy himself described the genesis of *Jude* in his preface. The first notes were made as early as 1887, and the book was written during 1892–4. (Hardy's memory was not always completely reliable on such matters, but there is no known reason to doubt this.) It was published serially in America (in *Harper's Weekly*) from December 1894 to November 1895: as in the case of *Tess*, the serial version was considerably bowdlerised and cut. It was published as a book by Osgood, McIlvaine and Co. on 1 November 1895 in England, and by Harper and Brothers later in the same month in America. Mrs Hardy, who was horrified at the book, did her best to prevent its publication by writing to, then going to see, Sir Richard Garnett. She was not, of course, the last to react in this way.

Harper's Weekly, 8 December 1894

❬ This remarkable page, a reply to the critical storm that had not yet broken out, appeared in the magazine which published *Jude* itself. Hardy had offered *Jude* to Harper with the assurance that 'it would not bring a blush to a school-girl's cheek'. Many years later Henry Harper wrote an account of what happened: 'It had not gone far before it looked a little squally to the editor, who wrote to Hardy about it. In answer, Hardy regretted that it was not the story which he had originally in mind when he approached us, but that the characters had taken things into their own hands and were doing better work than he anticipated. He advised us either to discontinue the story and put a note in the *Magazine* to the effect that it was not the tale we had contracted for; or he would give permission to the editor to delete any passages which he thought might be questioned by his readers. . . .' (Weber, *Hardy in America*, p. 92). Since it was the policy of the magazine not to publish anything which 'could not be read aloud in the home', the editor, Henry Alden, not only bowdlerised the novel but wrote a defence of Hardy's fiction that was really an indirect defence of the novel they were publishing.

Thomas Hardy

A new novel from Thomas Hardy is as eagerly awaited as one from George Eliot used to be, though with a more popular expectation than was awakened by this most thoughtful woman after she had left the field of common life so humorously and tragically represented in *Adam Bede* and *The Mill on the Floss*—novels nearer in kind to Mr. Hardy's than are found elsewhere in English fiction.

The first chapters of Mr. Hardy's new novel are already before the readers of HARPER'S MAGAZINE. In this first instalment the story is entitled 'The Simpletons'; hereafter it will appear under the caption of 'Hearts Insurgent.' Each title is significant of the author's main purpose, which is, as it always has been, to deal with simple hearts in the common conditions of human life—their aspirations in conflict with their passions, and their passions breaking and broken against the barriers of circumstance. In this new novel the interest is concentrated, more even than in *The Return of the Native* or *The Mayor of Casterbridge*, upon a masculine character and career; and, as in the latter of the novels just mentioned, the matrimonial entanglement is exacerbating.

A peculiar interest in this story is due to the fact that it is the immediate successor of *Tess of the D'Urbervilles*, a novel which deeply affected the hearts of its readers, because it was the tragedy of a human life, hopelessly entangled in the web which nature, society, and unhappy circumstances had combined to weave about a woman, to whom no efficient help (none that she could see or avail of) ever came for her release. Apart from the heart-breaking sorrow of the tale, as touching an individual life so unhappily situated and relentlessly conducted to its awful issues, this novel suggested important questions as to the proper province of art in its ethical relations, and as to the philosophy conveyed in so severe a view of what Mr. Hardy himself calls 'the grimness of the general human situation.'

No one could adduce from the novel a passage tending to corrupt good morals, since in the most emotional situations the author was singularly reticent, and he never wrote a sentence in any of his novels which panders to vicious tastes or inclinations. He introduced no mystical or preternatural elements to confuse or disguise the simple facts presented. No sensuous veil covered the frankness and directness of an appeal such as Prometheus made in the great tragedy of Æschylus.

The questions raised naturally led to a serious consideration of Mr. Hardy's previous novels—especially those of a tragic character —with reference to his general attitude toward subjects of the deepest human interest and solicitude.

To this consideration we shall presently revert, after a brief and necessarily inadequate view of the general scope and character of Mr. Hardy's fiction. The impressiveness of his work and its dramatic strength, the noble simplicity and classic reserve of his manner, and the living truth of every scene and every character in his stories have given him a unique position—all the more so because the motives of his novels have never been drawn from the world of books or closely associated with topics suggested by culture. His novels are not those of the study; their lines run in the free fields of nature, in an out-of-door atmosphere, and with that ready turn and flexion characteristic of all natural movements. He has never sought to illuminate any critical period of human history, as George Eliot did in *Romola*, or to treat some very complex strain of social life, as she did in *Middlemarch*. None of his works depends for its interest upon any 'burning' question of the day. The motives which inspired *Felix Holt, Alton Locke, Daniel Deronda*, or *Robert Elsmere* have never distracted him from his purpose—the portrayal of human life in simple conditions and lying next the bosom of Mother Earth. . . .

. . . In considering Mr. Hardy's moral attitude one must keep within the limits of the special field he has chosen for his work, and the only requirement we can make is for the whole truth of Wessex life as it is lived. The artist is only indirectly a philosopher or a preacher. He does not attempt to justify the ways of God to men, or to show how the ways of men may be finally reconciled to those of God; he attempts nothing beyond the concrete synthesis visible to him. He may, indeed, admit into his view so much of heaven's light and so much of Christian grace as it will bear—as Shakespeare did in *The Merchant of Venice*—but no more. We fail to see how Mr. Hardy could, without violence and confusion, have endowed his characters with qualities and given them experiences wholly out of keeping with their impulses and their environment and opportunity, or how he could have conducted his dramatic movements to issues not indicated in the natural sequence of things. Lady Macbeth might (in some other sequence) have been converted; Shylock might have yielded to the first appeal of Portia to his mercy rather than to her final decree of absolute justice; and King

Lear (himself an old King of Wessex) might have lived out his last days in the society of his faithful daughter, and Cordelia (as in Tate's mangled version of the play) might have escaped hanging—but where then would have been the truth or significance of these mighty dramas? So with Tess. The cup of happiness she must not drink. As Dowden says of Lear: 'He is grandly passive—played upon by the manifold forces of nature and society. And though he is in part delivered from his imperious self-will, and learns at last what true love is, and that it exists in the world, Lear passes away from our sight not in any mood of resignation, or faith, or illuminated peace, but in a piteous agony of yearning for that love which he has found only to lose forever.' There is a singular parallel to this tragedy in the fate of Tess. Though, like Lear, she is 'more sinned against than sinning,' she has this destiny, growing out of her relations to nature and society, that to the last she must be stretched upon the 'rack of this tough world,' and through the stress come into an abnormal state, though not the extreme of madness, in which she commits a brutal crime. From Stonehenge, and a glimpse of the happiness that might have been hers, she is brought to the scaffold. Even the final paragraph of the novel, '"Justice" was done, and the President of the Immortals (in Æschylean phrase) had ended his sport with Tess,' repeats, as Mr. Hardy has himself pointed out, Gloster's comment:

'As flies to wanton boys are we to the gods;
They kill us for their sport.'

But putting the comparison aside, what is it the objecting moralist would have? What more effective sermon—if one calls for a sermon—could Mr. Hardy have preached than this: showing that in the world-old dilemma of the human heart, on the one side driven by Nature, through passions which she urges on to excess, lest she should fail of her ends, and on the other side scourged by the conventions of a social order, and by a conscience assentient to that order, for the excess itself—the full obedience to nature becoming a moral transgression, no resolution of the apparent discord is possible from either side, from Nature or from the moral law? This demonstration might not satisfy the moralist who insists upon the possibility of an ethical resolution, and flounders, like Mr. Huxley, in his Romanes lecture, trying to find it; but it is in perfect accord with Christianity, which finds a reconcilement of the conflict in the principle of regeneration—transcending Nature in her renewal, and the law in its fulfilment, wherein it dies.

It is true that Mr. Hardy does not illustrate this resolution, but he attempts no other. He presents the problem in all its difficulty, relentlessly emphasizing the harshness of the contradictory elements. It is a true statement of the problem in living terms. The optimistic poet leaps easily from the stress of pain and travail to an ideal fruition, but in lives not open to the light illuminating his vision the stress must be borne to the bitter end. Mr. Hardy does not love to dwell upon the morose aspects of life, but he never abates the sorrow of a wretched plight. He passes no inflexible judgments upon Nature or society. Nature is both kind and cruel, and 'that cold accretion of mankind called the world' is in its units 'unformidable, and even pitiable.' In some of his comments there is a 'note of revolt' against conventional judgments that condemn the frail because society must fortify itself against the frailty, but he would not relax the force of laws framed merely on social expedients because Nature is unconscious of such laws. Convention is the sign of human concord, and if civilization be a revolt against Nature, as Rousseau falsely thought, it is one in whose cause we have pledged 'our lives, our fortunes, and our sacred honor.' Nevertheless, it has its evils, as Nature, to our partial vision, has hers—the harshness of its very justice—and if its grim outward necessities, based on human weakness, were accepted by us as essential in the heart of things, human or divine, the issues of life would be wholly hopeless. If this is the lesson of Mr. Hardy's novels, it is also that of the gospel. If to Tess, in the crisis of her career, there had come some better help than was offered by her agnostic and recreant lover, Angel Clare, her story would have had a very different termination. As it was, she was deprived of the consolations of an uncondemning Nature, but not brought to a real knowledge of the uncondemning Christ.   [H. M. ALDEN]

The Daily Telegraph, 1 November 1895

... The story is indeed a sad one, its prevailing gloom unrelieved throughout by any of those subtle touches of quaint provincial humour which illumined the pages of Mr. Hardy's preceding works of fiction. In every other respect the book may be unhesitatingly pronounced a masterpiece.

The Morning Post, 7 November 1895

To write a story of over five hundred pages, and longer by far than the majority of three-volume novels, without allowing one single ray of humour, or even of cheerfulness, to dispel for a moment the gloomy atmosphere of hopeless pessimism was no ordinary task, and might have taxed the powers of the most relentless observers of life. Even Euripides, had he been given to the writing of novels, might well have faltered before such a tremendous undertaking. But Mr. Thomas Hardy, in 'Jude the Obscure' (Osgood, McIlvaine and Co.) has not only made the attempt, but has come through the ordeal with flying colours, or rather, to use a more appropriate metaphor, with flags hoisted half-mast high. It is probable that somewhere or other we shall hear the 'inevitableness of the old Greek tragedy' referred to in connection with the book, and its sequence of unmitigated wretchedness; but inevitableness is precisely the quality which is wanting in 'Jude the Obscure,' except in so far that the author was determined everything should go wrong with everybody in the story, and that events fell out accordingly. The purpose of the work, for unless it is to be regarded as 'a novel with a purpose' it is hard to imagine why it should have been written at all, is, apparently, in the first place to illustrate a highly original theory that if you marry the wrong person you will probably be unhappy in your married life, and in the second place to show how strong may be the force of convention in upsetting the plans even of those who fancy that they are most emancipated. Such themes as Mr. Hardy now deals with have formed the motives of scores of short stories and not a few full-bodied novels, and it is not easy to see how anyone, no matter what his personal opinions on sociological questions and on the right of man to 'gang his ain gait,' can have supposed that any good object could be achieved by the putting-forth of such a farrago of miscellaneous miseries as is contained within the pages of this volume.

To clearly sketch the plot of the story within a reasonable space would not be an easy or, indeed, a possible task, nor is there any necessity to attempt it. Jude is an orphan of very humble origin, cursed with a yearning for that higher education of which we hear so much nowadays, and is, in fact, a most promising subject for University extension lectures. But everything goes wrong with him. To begin with, he is so extremely sensitive that 'he could scarcely bear to see trees cut down or lopped, from a fancy that it hurt them; and late pruning, when the sap was up and the tree bled profusely, had been a positive grief to him in his infancy.' Arrived at manhood, he falls an absurdly easy victim to the wiles of a coarse-grained girl, who introduces herself to his notice by the simple expedient of throwing a piece of greasy bacon at his face. 'Pigs,' as it is interesting to learn, 'were rather plentiful hereabout,

being bred and fattened in large numbers in certain parts of North
Wessex.' The chapters in which the entrapping of Jude is described
are surely among the most unsatisfactory ever perpetrated by any
novelist who could claim a prominent place among contemporary
writers. Not that they are much inferior to many others in the
book, if at all, but they could not well be worse than they are. Jude
and Arabella soon part, and the man, who is now a stonemason,
goes to Oxford, where he meets and falls in love with his cousin
Susanna Florence Mary Bridehead, commonly known as Sue. Sue,
though only a girl in a Church embroidery shop, is widely read in a
very special sense of the phrase. 'I have had advantages,' she says;
'I don't know Latin and Greek, though I know the grammars of
those tongues. But I know most of the Greek and Latin classics
through translations, and other books too. I read Lemprière,
Catullus, Martial, Juvenal, Lucian, Beaumont and Fletcher, Boc-
caccio, Scarron, De Brantôme, Sterne, De Foe, Smollett;' in fact her
reading was 'extensive and peculiar,' at any rate for a shop-girl of
nineteen or twenty years old. It was 'by accident' that she came to
read most of these books, an 'accident,' as the story shows, which
had a considerable bearing on the troubles and trials of Jude and
this unsatisfactory cousin. Sue is altogether a strange and unnatural creature. A highly-strung, nervous, hysterical woman, who
in the most tremendous crises of her life can quote poetry and
prose as calmly as a lecturer, is distinctly abnormal. No wonder
that the unhappy Phillotson, one of the least irrational of the personages in the story, writhes when his wife (in which capacity Sue
appears in the middle and again at the end of the book) throws
quotations from eminent economists at his head. '"What do I care
about J. S. Mill," moaned he, "I only want to lead a quiet life."'
But that, poor man, is exactly what Sue makes it impossible for
him to do. . . .

The Pall Mall Gazette, 12 November 1895
Jude the Obscene

'All you be a queer lot as husbands and wives,' said Arabella, in a
rare moment of reflectiveness; and we quite agree with her, though
we don't think that she had much right to speak, being certainly of
the queerest herself.

This was how it all came about. Jude, who had aspirations
towards culture and cathedral towns, took a country walk. Having
received in mid-face some strange fragment of a pig's anatomy
(that we prefer not to specify), he promptly fell in love with

Arabella, the thrower of the thing—a young woman of billowy attractions, a Cochin China complexion, and dimples deftly produced by artificial suction. But he only talked Greek philosophy to her till she, bent on capture by hook or by crook, rushed brightly upstairs, and Jude rushing after her was caught in the noose. For he was an honourable, though obscure, Jude, and when the itinerant pill-vendor was brought to bear upon him, and he found that the Cochin complexion was becoming streaky from emotion, and the dimples almost convex with despair, he gave up his cultured cathedral hopes and married her. So they lived in a lonely roadside cottage. But it didn't last long. 'A little chill overspread him at her first unrobing,' for he found that all her hair was movable, and then, too, he learned too much about those dimples; yet more, he discovered that the pathetic necessity for marriage had been a pure figment of her brain or tongue. And Arabella got annoyed with him too, because when the pig-killer was late Jude did the business badly, and so there was no blackpot. Also she found him dull. So after standing in the street on Sunday with hair (the barber's) dishevelled, bodice apart, and hands reeking with melted fat, she left for Australia, while he returned to his lodgings in a better mood and said his prayers.

After this he went to Christminster, the city of his dreams, and fell in love again with his cousin Sue, whose photograph he had been kissing on and off for years, and who had recently been turned out of an 'ecclesiastical warehouse' for keeping nude statues of Venus and Apollo wrapped up in brown paper in her bedroom. They confessed their love; but annoyed presumably at the discovery of a living legal impediment in the Antipodes, Sue abruptly married Phillotson, the elderly schoolmaster, and Jude, exclaiming as he worked, 'O Susanna Florence Mary, you don't know what marriage means,' was reduced to giving her away 'like a she-ass or she-goat, or any other domestic animal,' with a tea-kettle thrown in to start the pure home decently. But this didn't last long either, and after a brief interval of window-jumping and non-conjugal holding of hands, she decided that she was living in sin, quoted J. S. Mill, and departed to set up (cousinly) house with Jude.

Meanwhile Arabella has just stepped round again from Australia; and now our heads are whirling, and we feel quite incompetent to cope any more with the mixedness of it. All we know is that there are bigamies and divorces, and early infants alighting from distant lands. The cousinly establishment somehow ceases to be cousinly, in spite of the ineffectiveness of several nibblings at registry offices; each visit thither having failed at the last minute owing to Sue's fears of her love 'not being proof against the sordid conditions of a business contract.' And so in due course an unblessed family appears; and soon early and later infants are attracting momentary attention by hanging each other with box-cord on little pegs all round the room. After this come inquests, and remorse, and a new consciousness of sin, ending up in the re-marriage of all the divorcees, making, to the best of our reckoning, a total of six marriages and two obscenities to the count of two couples and a half—a record performance, we should think. And they all lived unhappily ever after, except Jude, who spat blood and died; while Arabella curled her hair with an umbrella stay and looked archly at her old acquaintance the itinerant quack.

To turn to serious criticism is to turn from laughter to tears; for to us who have admired and even loved Mr. Hardy in the past, this last production of him is worth a weeping, and but little more. It is indeed, as he himself tells us in his preface, a book of 'fret and fever, derision and disaster'—dirt, drivel, and damnation (these last characteristics he omits to catalogue). There is, as he promises, no mincing of the words in this his presentment of 'the tragedy of unfulfilled aims.' The 'series of seemings' stand forth in naked squalor and ugliness, shaped indeed by the hand of a master, but of a master in a nightmare. Of all the unlovely and unloveable characters Jude himself seems to us the least unlovely and the least obscure. He is, in truth, a fine conception, though marred and shadowed by an almost impossible weakness of will and wisdom. The gloomy whole is unrelieved to any material extent by the painting of country scenes, such as we have learned to expect from him who is, in spite of all, one of our greatest artists, when treating of that great, grave, gracious Wessex-land that he and we both love. In fact, we find little charm or merit in the book except that of the actual wording, which with him is never without potency.

So, Mr. Hardy, don't disappoint us again. Give us quickly another and a cleaner book to take the bad taste out of our mouths. Of this we can only say with red-eyed Widow Edlin, 'We can't stomach 'un.'

The Guardian, 13 November 1895

Mr. Hardy's new novel, *Jude the Obscure*, is a book of which it is not easy to discover the motive. It discusses the unpalatable question of sexual morality, and the author says in his Preface that he is 'not aware that there is anything in the handling to which exception can be taken.' This is a point upon which tastes differ, and our taste is very much offended by almost the whole book. It has two principal female characters—one revoltingly coarse, the other as revoltingly refined. The hero, Jude Fawley, is a limp, characterless creature, credited in the beginning with high-soaring aspirations after religion, and scholarship, and elevation to a more refined social world than he is born in. As a boy he is interesting and touching, but as a man contemptibly weak, unstable, and maundering. He is first awakened from dreams of books to thoughts of dalliance—we cannot call it love—by a blow on the ear from a 'soft, cold substance' flung at him as he is walking home from his work on a summer evening, thinking how 'he might become even a Bishop by leading a pure, energetic, wise, Christian life.' The 'soft cold substance' is a bit of raw pig's flesh, thrown at him in sport by Arabella Donn, a young country-woman, with whom he is not yet on speaking terms. Arabella's subsequent blandishments are in keeping with her first overture, and in a very short time she deliberately compromises herself with Jude in order to compel him to marry her. Their married life is what might be expected from such a courtship, and in less than a year they part. Susannah Bridehead —commonly called Sue—is the revoltingly refined heroine. In an odd way of her own she falls in love with her cousin Jude, but, Jude being married already, she engages herself to a schoolmaster eighteen years older than herself, whom she likes as a friend, but feels the greatest aversion to as a husband. During all the time of her engagement, and after her marriage, she carries on a very fidgetting, shilly-shally sort of flirtation with Jude, and finally asks and receives permission from her husband to go away and live with her lover. Ultimately she goes back to her lawful husband, who is as accommodating about her return as he was about her going away, and Arabella at the same time comes back to Jude. Both couples are miserable, and their misery is shown up in some brutal and thoroughly revolting chapters. Throughout the book a great many insulting things are said about marriage, religion, and all the obligations and relations of life which most people hold sacred. The circumstances of all the actors in the story are kept at a dead level of sordid commonness; and there is not a single character in the book that it is pleasant to dwell upon. Mr. Hardy has long taught us to expect much that is disagreeable and disquieting in his books, but generally the moral and physical ugliness is relieved by an admixture of beautiful and powerful scenes. But in this book there is very little power, hardly any beauty, and no discernible intention. It affects one like a shameful nightmare, which one only wishes to forget as quickly and as completely as possible.

The World, 13 November 1895
Hardy the Degenerate

Not many weeks ago the announcement that Mr. Thomas Hardy's new novel, in the course of its passage through the pages of *Harper's Magazine*, had been condensed and modified in the alleged interests of propriety moved us to utter a protest against the excesses of this bowdlerising spirit. We are reluctantly compelled to admit, now that *Jude the Obscure* (Osgood, McIlvaine) is published 'as originally written,' that the editor of the magazine in question cannot in any fairness be convicted of excessive 'pandering to Podsnap.' What he did in the main was to relieve Mr. Hardy's pages of realistic details which are not merely gratuitous, but disgusting. *Jude the Obscure*, says Mr. Hardy, is a novel 'addressed by a man to men and women of full age,' and, that being so, he holds himself exempted from the necessity of 'mincing' his words. Granted: but that is no excuse for demanding of his reader the gastric imperturbability of a well-seasoned pork-butcher. The opening scene of Jude's courtship of Arabella—we beg pardon, of Arabella's courtship of Jude—is enough to sicken a scavenger. As for the nauseating chapter devoted to the killing of the pig, it may best be described as an act of literary suicide. Perhaps, as the novel was primarily destined for an American audience, all this talk of chitterlings and 'innerds' was meant as a delicate compliment to the inhabitants of Porkopolis, Ohio. But we doubt whether the average full-grown British man or woman cares sufficiently for wading in pigstyes or shambles to appreciate Mr. Hardy's graphic and circumstantial delineation of the last hours and butchering of the obscure one's fatted porker. We are not so sure, however, that Mr. Hardy's Wessex peasants, especially that 'complete and substantial female human,' as he elegantly describes Jude's first sweetheart, are not even more swinish in their ways than his pigs. The frank animalism of Arabella's methods makes one almost regret the disappearance of the porcine *dramatis personæ* so early in the story. A pig, at any rate, if it makes no pretence to lead the higher life, is at least never morbid. And, so far as we are aware, there are no New or Obscure Pigs even in the kingdom of Wessex.

. . . Mr. Hardy, in short, seems to have become equally enamoured of the methods of Zola and Tolstoi—Zola of *La Terre*, and Tolstoi the decadent sociologist. It is a bad blend, and the results, as manifested in the volume before us, are anything but satisfactory. Humanity, as envisaged by Mr. Hardy, is largely compounded of hoggishness and hysteria. . . .

[JEANNETTE L. GILDER]

The Sun, 20 November 1895

Had 'Jude the Obscure' (Osgood, McIlvaine, and Co.) been the work of an artist less conscientious and sincere than Mr. Thomas Hardy, nothing could have saved it from condemnation. So sordid is the tale it sets forth, so unrelieved is the gloom of the incidents, and—to be frank—so unnecessarily coarse are certain of the details, that, were it not for the saving grace of the artist, and the evident purity of its motive, the whole thing would pass for a misdirected effort in decadent realism. Even as it is, illumined by Mr. Hardy's workmanship, and vitalised by its power, it remains a book that his sincerest admirers will wish unwritten—a book that can do no one of its readers any possible good, and may do to many of them incalculable harm. The artist who lends his countenance to the treatment of animal subjects does so under grave responsibility; and one can scarcely envy Mr. Hardy his self-imposed burthen. For 'Jude' is a serious responsibility to undertake. . . .

The Critic, 23 November 1895

For a Book by Thomas Hardy

With searching feet, through dark circuitous ways,
I plunged and stumbled; round me, far and near,
Quaint hordes of eyeless phantoms did appear,
Twisting and turning in a bootless chase,—
When, like an exile given by God's grace
To feel once more a human atmosphere,
I caught the world's first murmur, large and clear,
Flung from a singing river's endless race.

Then through a magic twilight from below,
I heard its grand sad song as in a dream:
Life's wild infinity of mirth and woe
It sang me; and, with many a changing gleam,
Across the music of its onward flow
I saw the cottage lights of Wessex beam.

EDWIN ARLINGTON ROBINSON

'Written before the appearance of *Hearts Insurgent*'
(note by the editors of *The Critic*)

Harper's Weekly, 7 December 1895

It has never been quite decided yet, I believe, just what is the kind
and what is the quality of pleasure we get from tragedy. A great
many people have said what it is, but they seem not to have said
this even to their own satisfaction. It is certain that we do get
pleasure from tragedy, and it is commonly allowed that the pleasure we get from tragedy is nobler than the pleasure we get from
comedy. An alloy of any such pleasure as we get from comedy is
held to debase this finer emotion, but this seems true only as to the
whole effect of tragedy. The Greek tragedy kept itself purely
tragic; the English tragedy assimilated all elements of comedy and
made them tragic; so that in the end Hamlet and Macbeth are as
high sorrowful as Orestes and Œdipus.

I.

I should be rather ashamed of lugging the classic and the romantic in here, if it were not for the sense I have of the return of an
English writer to the Greek motive of tragedy in a book which
seems to me one of the most tragical I have read. I have always
felt in Mr. Thomas Hardy a charm which I have supposed to be that
of the elder pagan world, but this I have found in his lighter moods,
for the most part, and chiefly in his study of the eternal-womanly,
surviving in certain unconscienced types and characters from a
time before Christianity was, and more distinctly before Puritanism was. Now, however, in his latest work he has made me feel
our unity with that world in the very essence of his art. He has
given me the same pity and despair in view of the blind struggles of
his modern English lower-middle-class people that I experience
from the destinies of the august figures of Greek fable. I do not
know how instinctively or how voluntarily he has appealed to our
inherent superstition of Fate, which used to be a religion; but I am
sure that in the world where his hapless people have their being,
there is not only no Providence, but there is Fate alone; and the
environment is such that character itself cannot avail against it.
We have back the old conception of an absolutely subject humanity
unguided and unfriended. The gods, careless of mankind, are
again over all; only, now, they call themselves conditions.

The story is a tragedy, and tragedy almost unrelieved by the
humorous touch which the poet is master of. The grotesque is there
abundantly, but not the comic; and at times this ugliness heightens
the pathos to almost intolerable effect. But I must say that the
figure of Jude himself is, in spite of all his weakness and debase-
ment, one of inviolable dignity. He is the sport of fate, but he is

never otherwise than sublime; he suffers more for others than for himself. The wretched Sue who spoils his life and her own, helplessly, inevitably, is the kind of fool who finds the fool in the poet and prophet so often, and brings him to naught. She is not less a fool than Arabella herself; though of such exaltation in her folly that we cannot refuse her a throe of compassion, even when she is most perverse. All the characters, indeed, have the appealing quality of human creatures really doing what they must while seeming to do what they will. It is not a question of blaming them or praising them; they are in the necessity of what they do and what they suffer. One may indeed blame the author for presenting such a conception of life; one may say that it is demoralizing if not immoral; but as to his dealing with his creations in the circumstance which he has imagined, one can only praise him for his truth.

The story has to do with some things not hitherto touched in fiction, or Anglo-Saxon fiction at least; and there cannot be any doubt of the duty of criticism to warn the reader that it is not for all readers. But not to affirm the entire purity of the book in these matters would be to fail of another duty of which there can be as little doubt. I do not believe any one can get the slightest harm from any passage of it; only one would rather that innocence were not acquainted with all that virtue may know. Vice can feel nothing but self-abhorrence in the presence of its facts.

II.

The old conventional personifications seem drolly factitious in their reference to the vital reality of this strange book. I suppose it can be called morbid, and I do not deny that it is. But I have not been able to find it untrue, while I know that the world is full of truth that contradicts it. The common experience, or perhaps I had better say the common knowledge of life contradicts it. Commonly, the boy of Jude's strong aspiration and steadfast ambition succeeds and becomes in some measure the sort of man he dreamed of being. Commonly, a girl like Sue flutters through the anguish of her harassed and doubting youth and settles into acquiescence with the ordinary life of women, if not acceptance of it. Commonly, a boy like the son of Jude, oppressed from birth with the sense of being neither loved nor wanted, hardens himself against his misery, fights for the standing denied him, and achieves it. The average Arabella has no reversion to her first love when she has freed herself from it. The average Phillotson does not give up his wife to the man she says she loves, and he does not take her back knowing her loathing

for himself. I grant all these things; and yet the author makes me
believe that all he says to the contrary inevitably happened.

I allow that there are many displeasing things in the book, and
few pleasing. Arabella's dimple-making, the pig-killing, the boy
suicide and homicide; Jude's drunken second marriage; Sue's wilful
self-surrender to Phillotson; these and other incidents are revolting.
They make us shiver with horror and grovel with shame, but we
know that they are deeply founded in the condition, if not in the
nature of humanity. There are besides these abhorrent facts certain accusations against some accepted formalities of civilization,
which I suppose most readers will find hardly less shocking. But I
think it is very well for us to ask from time to time the reasons of
things, and to satisfy ourselves, if we can, what the reasons are. If
the experience of Jude with Arabella seems to arraign marriage,
and it is made to appear not only ridiculous but impious that two
young, ignorant, impassioned creatures should promise lifelong
fealty and constancy when they can have no real sense of what
they are doing, and that then they should be held to their rash vow
by all the forces of society, it is surely not the lesson of the story
that any other relation than marriage is tolerable for the man and
woman who live together. Rather it enforces the conviction that
marriage is the sole solution of the question of sex, while it shows
how atrocious and heinous marriage may sometimes be.

III.

I find myself defending the book on the ethical side when I
meant chiefly to praise it for what seems to me its artistic excellence. It has not only the solemn and lofty effect of a great tragedy;
a work far faultier might impart this; but it has unity very uncommon in the novel, and especially the English novel. So far as I
can recall its incidents there are none but such as seem necessary
from the circumstances and the characters. Certain little tricks
which the author sometimes uses to help himself out, and which
give the sense of insincerity or debility, are absent here. He does
not invoke the playful humor which he employs elsewhere. Such
humor as there is tastes bitter, and is grim if not sardonic. This
tragedy of fate suggests the classic singleness of means as well as the
classic singleness of motive.   W. D. HOWELLS

Cosmopolis, January 1896

... It is a study of four lives, a rectangular problem in failures,
drawn with almost mathematical rigidity. The tragedy of these

four persons is constructed in a mode almost as geometrical as that
in which Dr. Samuel Clarke was wont to prove the existence of the
Deity. It is difficult not to believe that the author set up his four
ninepins in the wilds of Wessex, and built up his theorem round
them. Here is an initial difficulty. Not quite thus is theology or
poetry conveniently composed; we like to conceive that the relation of the parts was more spontaneous, we like to feel that the
persons of a story have been thrown up in a jet of enthusiasm, not
put into a cave of theory to be slowly covered with stalactite.

'Jude the Obscure' is acted in North Wessex (Berkshire) and
just across the frontier, at Christminster (Oxford), which is not in
Wessex at all. We want our novelist back among the rich orchards
of the Hintocks, and where the water-lilies impede the lingering
river at Shottsford Ash. Berkshire is an unpoetical county, 'meanly
utilitarian,' as Mr. Hardy confesses; the imagination hates its
concave, loamy cornfields and dreary, hedgeless highways. The
local history has been singularly tampered with in Berkshire; it is
useless to speak to us of ancient records where the past is all
obliterated, and the thatched and dormered houses replaced by
modern cottages. In choosing North Wessex as the scene of a novel
Mr. Hardy wilfully deprives himself of a great element of his
strength. Where there are no prehistoric monuments, no ancient
buildings, no mossed and immemorial woodlands, he is Samson
shorn. In Berkshire, the change which is coming over England so
rapidly, the resignation of the old dreamy elements of beauty, has
proceeded further than anywhere else in Wessex. Pastoral loveliness is to be discovered only here and there, while in Dorsetshire it
still remains the master-element. All this combines to lessen the
physical charm of 'Jude the Obscure' to those who turn from it in
memory to 'Far from the Madding Crowd' and 'The Return of the
Native.'

But, this fortuitous absence of beauty being acknowledged, the
novelist's hand shows no falling off in the vigour and reality of his
description. It may be held, in fact, to be a lesser feat to raise
before us an enchanting vision of the valley of the Froom, than
successfully to rivet our attention on the prosaic arable land en-
circling the dull hamlet of Marygreen.

To pass from the landscape to the persons, two threads of action
seem to be intertwined in 'Jude the Obscure.' We have, first of all,
the contrast between the ideal life the young peasant of scholarly
instincts wished to lead, and the squalid real life into which he was
fated to sink. We have, secondly, the almost rectilinear puzzle of
the sexual relations of the four principal characters. Mr. Hardy has

wished to show how cruel destiny can be to the eternal dream of youth, and he has undertaken to trace the lamentable results of unions in a family exhausted by intermarriage and poverty. Some collision is apparent between these aims; the first seems to demand a poet, the second a physician. The Fawleys are a decayed and wasted race, in the last of whom, Jude, there appears, with a kind of flicker in the socket, a certain intellectual and artistic brightness. In favourable surroundings, we feel that this young man might have become fairly distinguished as a scholar, or as a sculptor. But at the supreme moment, or at each supreme moment, the conditions hurl him back into insignificance. When we examine clearly what these conditions are, we find them to be instinctive. He is just going to develop into a lad of education, when Arabella throws her hideous missile at him, and he sinks with her into a resigned inferiority.

So far, the critical court is with Mr. Hardy; these scenes and their results give a perfect impression of truth. Later on, it is not quite evident whether the claim on Jude's passions, or the inherent weakness of his inherited character, is the source of his failure. Perhaps both. But it is difficult to see what part Oxford has in his destruction, or how Mr. Hardy can excuse the rhetorical diatribes against the university which appear towards the close of the book. Does the novelist really think that it was the duty of the heads of houses to whom Jude wrote his crudely pathetic letters to offer him immediately a fellowship? We may admit to the full the pathos of Jude's position—nothing is more heart-rending than the obscurity of the half-educated—but surely, the fault did not lie with Oxford.

The scene at Commemoration (Part VI.) is of a marvellous truth and vividness of presentment, but it would be stronger, and even more tragic, if Mr. Hardy did not appear in it as an advocate taking sides with his unhappy hero. In this portion of his work, it seems to me, Mr. Hardy had but to paint—as clearly and as truthfully as he could—the hopes, the struggles, the disappointments of Jude, and of these he has woven a tissue of sombre colouring, indeed, and even of harsh threads, but a tapestry worthy of a great imaginative writer. It was straightforward poet's work in invention and observation, and he has executed it well.

. . . It does not appear to me that we have any business to call in question the right of a novelist of Mr. Hardy's extreme distinction to treat what themes he will. We may wish—and I for my part cordially wish—that more pleasing, more charming plots than this could take his fancy. But I do not feel at liberty to challenge his discretion. One thing, however, the critic of comparative literature must note. We have, in such a book as 'Jude the Obscure,' traced the full circle of propriety. A hundred and fifty years ago, Fielding and Smollett brought up before us pictures, used expressions, described conduct, which appeared to their immediate successors a little more crude than general reading warranted. In Miss Burney's hands and in Miss Austin's, the morals were still further hedged about. Scott was even more daintily reserved. We came at last to Dickens, where the clamorous passions of mankind, the coarser accidents of life, were absolutely ignored, and the whole question of population seemed reduced to the theory of the gooseberry bush. This was the *ne plus ultra* of decency; Thackeray and George Eliot relaxed this intensity of prudishness; once on the turn, the tide flowed rapidly, and here is Mr. Hardy ready to say any mortal thing that Fielding said, and a good deal more too.

So much we note, but to censure it, if it calls for censure, is the duty of the moralist and not the critic. Criticism asks how the thing is done, whether the execution is fine and convincing. To tell so squalid and so abnormal a story in an interesting way is in itself a feat, and this, it must be universally admitted, Mr. Hardy has achieved. 'Jude the Obscure' is an irresistible book; it is one of those novels into which we descend and are carried on by a steady impetus to the close, when we return, dazzled, to the light of common day. The two women, in particular, are surely created by a master. Every impulse, every speech, which reveals to us the coarse and animal, but not hateful Arabella, adds to the solidity of her portrait. We may dislike her, we may hold her intrusion into our consciousness a disagreeable one, but of her reality there can be no question: Arabella lives.

It is conceivable that not so generally will it be admitted that Sue Bridehead is convincing. Arabella is the excess of vulgar normality; every public bar and village fair knows Arabella, but Sue is a strange and unwelcome product of exhaustion. The *vita sexualis* of Sue is the central interest of the book, and enough is told about it to fill the specimen tables of a German specialist. Fewer testimonies will be given to her reality than to Arabella's because hers is much the rarer case. But her picture is not less admirably drawn; Mr. Hardy has, perhaps, never devoted so much care to the portrait of a woman. She is a poor, maimed 'degenerate,' ignorant of herself and of the perversion of her instincts, full of febrile, amiable illusions, ready to dramatise her empty life, and play at loving though she cannot love. Her adventure with the undergraduate has not taught her what she is; she quits Phillotson still ignorant of the source of her repulsion; she lives with Jude, after a long, agonising struggle, in a relation that she accepts with distaste, and when the tragedy comes, and her children are killed, her poor extravagant brain slips one grade further down, and she sees in this calamity the chastisement of God. What has she done to be chastised? She does not know, but supposes it must be her abandonment of Philottson, to whom, in a spasm of self-abasement, and shuddering with repulsion, she returns without a thought for the misery of Jude. It is a terrible study in pathology, but of the splendid success of it, of the sustained intellectual force implied in the evolution of it, there cannot, I think, be two opinions.

One word must be added about the speech of the author and of the characters in 'Jude the Obscure.' Is it too late to urge Mr. Hardy to struggle against the jarring note of rebellion which seems growing upon him? It sounded in 'Tess,' and here it is, more roughly expressed, further acerbated. What has Providence done to Mr. Hardy that he should rise up in the arable land of Wessex and shake his fist at his Creator? He should not force his talent, should not give way to these chimerical outbursts of philosophy falsely so called. His early romances were full of calm and lovely pantheism; he seemed in them to feel the deep-hued country landscapes full of rural gods, all homely and benign. We wish he would go back to Egdon Heath and listen to the singing in the heather. . . .

A fact about the infancy of Mr. Hardy has escaped the interviewers and may be recorded here. On the day of his birth, during a brief absence of his nurse, there slipped into the room an ethereal creature, known as the Spirit of Plastic Beauty. Bending over the cradle she scattered roses on it, and as she strewed them she blessed the babe. 'He shall have an eye to see moral and material loveliness, he shall speak of richly-coloured pastoral places in the accent of Theocritus, he shall write in such a way as to cajole busy men into a sympathy with old, unhappy, far-off things.' She turned and went, but while the nurse still delayed, a withered termagant glided into the room. From her apron she dropped toads among the rose-leaves, and she whispered: 'I am the genius of False Rhetoric, and led by me he shall say things ugly and coarse, not recognising them to be so, and shall get into a rage about matters that call for philosophic calm, and shall spoil some of his best passages with pedantry and incoherency. He shall not know what things belong to his peace, and he shall plague his most loyal admirers with the barbaric contortions of his dialogue.' So saying, she put out her snaky tongue at the unoffending babe, and ever since, his imagination, noble as it is, and attuned to the great harmonies of nature, is liable at a moment's notice to give a shriek of discord. The worst, however, which any honest critic can say of 'Jude the Obscure' is that the fairy godmother seems, for the moment, to have relaxed her guardianship a little unduly.   EDMUND GOSSE

Letter from Hardy to Edmund Gosse, 10 November 1895

Max Gate
Dorchester
November 10th 1895

My Dear Gosse,

Your review is the most discriminating that has yet appeared. It required an artist to see that the plot is almost geometrically constructed—I ought not to say *constructed*, for, beyond a certain point, the characters necessitated it, and I simply let it come. As for the story itself, it is really sent out to those into whose souls the iron has entered, and has entered deeply at some time of their lives. But one cannot choose one's readers.

It is curious that some of the papers should look upon the novel as a manifesto on 'the marriage question' (although, of course, it involves it), seeing that it is concerned first with the labours of a poor student to get a University degree, and secondly with the tragic issues of two bad marriages, owing in the main to a doom or curse of hereditary temperament peculiar to the family of the parties. The only remarks which can be said to bear on the *general* marriage question occur in dialogue, and comprise no more than half a dozen pages in a book of five hundred. And of these remarks I state (p. 362) that my own views are not expressed therein. I suppose the attitude of these critics is to be accounted for by the accident that during the serial publication of my story, a sheaf of 'purpose' novels on the matter appeared.

You have hardly an idea how poor and feeble the book seems to me, as executed, beside the idea of it that I had formed in prospect.

I have received some interesting letters about it already—yours not the least so. Swinburne writes, too enthusiastically for me to quote with modesty.

Believe me, with sincerest thanks for your review,

Ever yours,
T H

P.S. One thing I did not answer. The 'grimy' features of the story go to show the contrast between the ideal life a man wished to lead, and the squalid real life he was fated to lead. The throwing of the pizzle, at the supreme moment of his young dream, is to sharply initiate the contrast. But I must have lamentably failed, as I feel I have, if this requires explanation and is not self-evident. The idea was meant to run all through the novel. It is, in fact, to be discovered in *every*body's life, though it lies less on the surface perhaps than it does in my poor puppet's.

T H

Letter from Thomas Hardy to Edmund Gosse, 20 November 1895

MAX GATE,
DORCHESTER,
November 20th, 1895.

I am keen about the new magazine. How interesting that you should be writing this review for it! I wish the book were more worthy of such notice and place.

You are quite right; there is nothing perverted or depraved in Sue's nature. The abnormalism consists in disproportion, not in inversion, her sexual instinct being healthy as far as it goes, but unusually weak and fastidious. Her sensibilities remain painfully alert notwithstanding, as they do in nature with such women. One point illustrating this I could not dwell upon: that, though she has children, her intimacies with Jude have never been more than occasional, even when they were living together (I mention that they occupy separate rooms, except towards the end), and one of her reasons for fearing the marriage ceremony is that she fears it would be breaking faith with Jude to withhold herself at pleasure, or altogether, after it; though while uncontracted she feels at liberty to yield herself as seldom as she chooses. This has tended to keep his passion as hot at the end as at the beginning, and helps to break his heart. He has never really possessed her as freely as he desired.

Sue is a type of woman which has always had an attraction for me, but the difficulty of drawing the type has kept me from attempting it till now.

Of course the book is all contrasts—or was meant to be in its original conception. Alas, what a miserable accomplishment it is, when I compare it with what I meant to make it!—*e.g.* Sue and her heathen gods set against Jude's reading the Greek testament; Christminster academical, Christminster in the slums; Jude the saint, Jude the sinner; Sue the Pagan, Sue the saint; marriage, no marriage; &c., &c.

As to the 'coarse' scenes with Arabella, the battle in the school-room, etc., the newspaper critics might, I thought, have sneered at them for their Fieldingism rather than for their Zolaism. But your everyday critic knows nothing of Fielding. I am read in Zola very little, but have felt akin locally to Fielding, so many of his scenes having been laid down this way, and his home near.

Did I tell you I feared I should seem too High-Churchy at the end of the book where Sue recants? You can imagine my surprise at some of the reviews.

What a self-occupied letter!

Ever sincerely,

T. H.

The Illustrated London News, 11 January 1896

The reader closes this book with a feeling that a huge pall has blotted out all the light of humanity. In one way, that sensation is a tribute to Mr. Hardy's mastery of his art. He has carried you from one broken hope to another, through a series of painful climaxes; and such is the spaciousness which his grasp of elemental things imparts to the story that a tragedy of three lives seems to fill the world with sorrow, and invite irony from the heavens. In 'Jude,' even more than in 'Tess,' Nature plays a sort of ironical chorus; the most casual circumstances fall into the dismal harmony of fate: an organ peals a hymn of gratitude at the very moment when Jude finds his children dead; and the first conversation that reaches his tortured ear from the street is between two parsons who are dis-cussing the eastward position. The humour which glances through most of Mr. Hardy's books—a humour which is never boisterous and not always genial, but still akin to the buoyancy of life—is here subdued to an undercurrent of grim mockery. 'Weddings be funerals 'a believe nowadays,' remarks the widow Edlin concerning one of the matrimonial adventures in the story. 'Fifty-four years ago, come Fall, since my man and I married. Times have changed since then.' That is amusing; but it does not kindle you to mirth. There is a child, a terrible little elf, Jude's boy by his first marriage, with 'an octogenarian's face,' set in listless indifference to the sur-face of things which usually engages a child's attention, with a deep and brooding pessimism which seems to have grown with him out of the cradle. It is upon this gruesome fragment of humanity, and not upon his father, that the burden of life falls most heavily.

'Little Father Time,' as the child is nick-named, observes the arrival of other children with disapproval and alarm. There are three in all, and when little Jude learns from Sue, the mother of two, that a fourth is expected, he breaks into reproaches, murders his two brothers, and hangs himself. Now, up to this point, woe has been heaped upon woe, and the reader has accepted it all, with some reservations, as a natural evolution of the circumstances. The tragedy of the children strains his belief to snapping point; and then comes a perfectly superfluous touch which snaps it altogether. Jude reports to the suffering mother of two of the dead little ones the opinion of the doctor, who, oddly enough, happens to be 'an advanced man.' He is so 'advanced' as to assure the father that unnatural children who murder their brothers and commit suicide are becoming common, owing to the 'universal wish not to live.' This is too much. Fortunately, it comes so near the end that the extraordinary power and even beauty of the book are not destroyed; but it is strange that Mr. Hardy did not perceive how he had imperilled the whole fabric by a stroke which passes the border of burlesque. The horror of the infant pessimist is changed in a moment to ghastly farce by this inopportune generalisation of the 'advanced' doctor. We all know perfectly well that baby Schopenhauers are not coming into the world in shoals. Children whose lives, stunted by poverty or disease, have acquired a gravity beyond their years, may be found everywhere in the overcrowded centres of population; but such a portrait as little Jude Fawley, who advocates the annihilation of the species, and gives a practical example of it at a tender age, does not present itself as typical of a devouring philosophy.

The immediate effect of this error in Mr. Hardy's scheme of all-embracing tribulation is that the reader renews his 'will to live' and be moderately cheerful, and is not at all disposed to take very seriously the final permutations of the conjugal tie which has played such pranks throughout the novel. Jude begins the real business of life by marrying Arabella, a coarse young woman of his rural district. That enterprise is a speedy failure, and Arabella goes off to Australia, where she commits bigamy, while Jude yields to the enchantments of his cousin Sue. Sue, however, marries Phillotson, the schoolmaster, and finding that match insupportable, rejoins Jude with her husband's consent. Arabella returns, and then there is a general divorcing. Jude divorces his wife; the schoolmaster divorces his. Arabella re-marries the bigamist, but Jude and Sue, after various unsuccessful expeditions to the registry-office and the church, decide that marriage is a mistake. After the death of her children, Sue, hitherto a most philosophical lady, much given to quoting Mill and Humboldt, is suddenly seized by a fit of what she calls renunciation. In this frame of mind she insists on returning to Phillotson, who marries her again. The deserted Jude takes to strong liquor, in which he falls a victim to Arabella, now a widow, who re-marries him. After a last despairing interview with his Sue, he dies. The perpetual shuffling of partners hovers dangerously near the ridiculous, though, to be sure, it seems Mr. Hardy's intent to show us what a tragi-comedy is the matrimonial bond, of which 'the letter killeth,' while the spirit is the sport of the whimsical humour of Nature. We may be rather staggered by the self-denial of the schoolmaster who, at the cost of his own social ruin, allows his most attractive and most perplexing wife to go her ways with her lover; but Sue, with all her pedantry, and in spite of the too evident efforts to focus in her all the restless imaginings of our modern adventurous womanhood, is an intensely vivid personality. When the pedantry is sloughed off, when she no longer 'talks profound,' when the blow of the children's tragic end to her nervous system plunges her into a reaction, and makes her regard her broken marriage with Phillotson as a sacramental obligation, which must be renewed at the price of even greater suffering—then, it is possible, Sue is more unreal than ever to many students of her career, and more truly feminine to many more. As for Jude, the young stone-cutter, whose soul, laden with theology, appeals vainly to the heads of colleges, while his body is doomed to manual labour, drink, and Arabella, he may strike us now and then as phantasmal. But read the story how you will, it is manifestly a work of genius, moving amid ideas and emotions of so large a significance that most of our fiction is to 'Jude the Obscure' as a hamlet to a hemisphere.

Blackwood's Magazine, January 1896
The Anti-Marriage League

... This inclination towards the treatment of subjects hitherto considered immoral or contrary to good manners, in the widest sense of the words—and the disposition to place what is called the Sex-question above all others as the theme of fiction—has gradually acquired the importance of a *parti pris*. It may be said that this question has always been the leading subject of romance; but this never in the sense of the words as now used. Love has been the subject of romance, and all the obstacles that have always come in its way, and the devotion and faithfulness of Lovers, the chosen Two, the perennial hero and heroine in whom the simpler ideals of life have been concentrated. What is now freely discussed as the physical part of the question, and treated as the most important, has hitherto been banished from the lips of decent people, and as much as possible from their thoughts; but is now freely given forth as the favourite subject for the chatter of girls, who no doubt in a great number of cases know nothing about what they are talking of, and therefore are more or less to be pardoned for following a hideous fashion which has the never-exhausted charm of shocking and startling everybody around. Indeed one of the things most conspicuous in this new method is the curious development of shameless Innocence, more dangerous than folly, more appalling almost than vice, because one does not know at any moment into what miserable quagmire its bold and ignorant feet may stumble. . . .

. . . Nothing, I think, but a theory could explain the wonderful want of perception which induces a man full of perceptions to make a mistake so fundamental; but it is done—and thus unconsciously affords us the strangest illustration of what Art can come to when given over to the exposition of the unclean. The present writer does not pretend to a knowledge of the works of Zola, which perhaps she ought to have before presuming to say that nothing so coarsely indecent as the whole history of Jude in his relations with his wife Arabella has ever been put in English print—that is to say, from the hands of a Master. There may be books more disgusting, more impious as regards human nature, more foul in detail, in those dark corners where the amateurs of filth find garbage to their taste; but not, we repeat, from any Master's hand. . . .

We can with difficulty guess what is Mr Hardy's motive in portraying such a struggle. It can scarcely be said to be one of those attacks upon the institution of Marriage, which is the undisguised inspiration of some of the other books before us. It is marriage indeed which in the beginning works Jude's woe; and it is by marriage, or rather the marrying of himself and others, that his end is brought about. We rather think the author's object must be, having glorified women by the creation of Tess, to show after all what destructive and ruinous creatures they are, in general circumstances and in every development, whether brutal or refined. Arabella, the first—the pig-dealer's daughter, whose native qualities have been ripened by the experiences of a barmaid—is the Flesh, unmitigated by any touch of human feeling except that of merciless calculation as to what will be profitable for herself. She is the native product of the fields, the rustic woman, exuberant and

overflowing with health, vanity, and appetite. The colloquy between her and her fellows in their disgusting work, after her first
almost equally disgusting interview with Jude, is one of the most
unutterable foulness—a shame to the language in which it is
recorded and suggested; and the picture altogether of the country
lasses at their outdoor work is more brutal in depravity than anything which the darkest slums could bring forth, as are the scenes
in which their good advice is carried out. Is it possible that there
are readers in England to whom this infamy can be palatable, and
who, either in inadvertence or in wantonness, can *make it pay*? Mr
Hardy informs us he has taken elaborate precautions to secure the
double profit of the serial writer, by subduing his colours and
diminishing his effects, in the presence of the less corrupt, so as to
keep the perfection of filthiness for those who love it. It would be
curious to compare in this unsavoury traffic how much of the
sickening essence of his story Mr Hardy has thought his first public
could stomach, and how many edifying details he has put in for the
enlightenment of those who have no squeamish scruples to get over.
The transaction is insulting to the public, with whom he trades the
viler wares under another name, with all the suppressed passages
restored, as old-book dealers say in their catalogues, recommending
their ancient scandal to the amateurs of the unclean. It is not the
first time Mr Hardy has adopted this expedient. If the English
public supports him in it, it will be to the shame of every individual
who thus confesses himself to like and accept what the author himself acknowledges to be unfit for the eyes—not of girls and young
persons only, but of the ordinary reader,—the men and women who
read the Magazines, the public whom we address in these pages.
That the prophets should prophesy falsely is not the most important fact in national degradation: it is only when the people love
to have it so that the climax is attained.

The other woman—who makes virtue vicious by keeping the
physical facts of one relationship in life in constant prominence by
denying, as Arabella does by satisfying them, and even more skil-
fully and insistently than Arabella—the fantastic *raisonneuse*,
Susan, completes the circle of the unclean. . . . This woman we are
required to accept as the type of high-toned purity. It is the women
who are the active agents in all this unsavoury imbroglio: the story
is carried on, and life is represented as carried on, entirely by their
means. The men are passive, suffering, rather good than otherwise, victims of these and of fate. Not only do they never dominate,
but they are quite incapable of holding their own against these
remorseless ministers of destiny, these determined operators,

managing all the machinery of life so as to secure their own way. This is one of the most curious developments of recent fiction. It is perhaps natural that it should be more or less the case in books written by women, to whom the mere facility of representing their their own sex acts as a primary reason for giving them the chief place in the scene. But it has now still more markedly, though much less naturally, become the method with men, in the hands of many of whom women have returned to the *rôle* of the temptress given to them by the old monkish sufferers of ancient times, who fled to the desert, like Anthony, to get free of them, but even there barely escaped with their lives from the seductions of the sirens, who were so audacious as to follow them to the very scene of the macerations and miseries into which the unhappy men plunged to escape from their toils. In the books of the younger men, it is now the woman who seduces—it is no longer the man.

This, however, is a consideration by the way. I have said that it is not clear what Mr Hardy's motive is in the history of Jude: but, on reconsideration, it becomes more clear that it is intended as an assault on the stronghold of marriage, which is now beleaguered on every side. The motto is, 'The letter killeth'; and I presume this must refer to the fact of Jude's early and unwilling union to Arabella, and that the lesson the novelist would have us learn is, that if marriage were not exacted, and people were free to form connections as the spirit moves them, none of these complications would have occurred, and all would have been well. 'There seemed to him, vaguely and dimly, something wrong in a social ritual which made necessary the cancelling of well-formed schemes involving years of thought and labour, of foregoing a man's one opportunity of showing himself superior to the lower animals, and of contributing his units of work to the general progress of his generation, because of a momentary surprise by a new and transitory instinct which had nothing in it of the nature of vice, and could be only at the most called weakness.' This is the hero's own view of the circumstances which, in obedience to the code of honour prevalent in the country-side, compelled his marriage. Suppose, however, that instead of upsetting the whole framework of society, Jude had shown himself superior to the lower animals by not yielding to that new and transitory influence, the same result could have been easily attained: and he might then have met and married Susan and lived happy ever after, without demanding a total overthrow of all existing laws and customs to prevent him from being unhappy. Had it been made possible for him to have visited Arabella as long as the new and transitory influence lasted,

9

and then to have lived with Susan as long as she pleased to permit him to do so, which was the best that could happen were marriage abolished, how would that have altered the circumstances? When Susan changed her mind would he have been less unhappy? when Arabella claimed him again would he have been less weak? ...

M.O.W.O.   [MRS OLIPHANT]

The Bookman (London), January 1896

After you have read 'Jude the Obscure,' your thoughts run in two separate channels cut by Mr. Hardy's two nearly separate purposes. Your opinion of the book will largely depend on which you regard as the main one. These purposes are wound in with the history of Jude and the history of Sue. Their histories are intertwined, but they are not quite inevitable to each other; and so, to a greater extent than in most tragedies, you can regard the two chief actors separately.

A work of the intensest human interest, it is not evenly strong: it has been written too much under the stress of feeling for that. Any discontent which is not roused by merely superficial causes, which is not finnicking, and any offence which the book may contain for timid readers, must arise, I think, from the story of Sue. Personally I feel no offence, and I speak for at least some women. But I am not sure if her championship might not have been bettered. In herself, she is one of Mr. Hardy's stimulating women. He is particularly anxious not to shirk the consequences of her temperament, of that free spirit of hers that gave so willingly when not coerced by laws and authority. But in exhibiting the results of this temperament acting on her circumstances—her shilly-shallying, her contrariness about the marriage tie—there is an amount of exaggeration, or of reiteration, that becomes nearly absurd, as did the fickleness in the hero of 'The Pursuit of the Well-Beloved.' There is here something more than the 'series of seemings, or personal impressions,' spoken of in the preface. There is downright propaganda, which is always unconvincing, and even loosening to the convictions of the already converted. Sue is a woman that excites and leads. She is influential; her opinions and feelings do not need much emphasis and repetition. When they are given these, she becomes too much of a pamphlet and platform victim of the cruel marriage bond. Sue could love, and was not well fitted for marriage life. There she is not so very abnormal, and this would be the sooner admitted had Mr. Hardy not taken so much trouble to justify her running to and fro between Phillotson and Jude. But I

admit this is a cold reception to a warm protest; and the fault of
the novelist one may readily forgive to the man of feeling, sending
his chivalry bravely out in new directions.

But the book is not made up of theories and examples of theories.
The title is truly descriptive. Jude is the real subject; and Jude's
story is among the most notable of Mr. Hardy's work. In his
greater books—and this is one, undoubtedly—he has a way of
passionately identifying himself with the aims or the sorrows of
one personage, whom he loves in his blackest, his sinfullest, his
pitifullest moments. That he does so, and that he does not hide
such moments, make him one of the very grimmest and most
sympathetic of all novelists. Tess, the Mayor, Clym Yeobright, and
now Jude, are of the company. Jude's history is written as life
writes a history, some features being traced from the beginning,
while later, from hitherto unstirred depths, circumstance calls up
the others. He is a man with the defects of his amiable virtues and
his sensitive nature. There is only one woman in the world for his
love and reverence, but if she be not there, his loneliness may seek
less good company. In strong drink he has sometimes found a
refuge from overtaxed nerves. Life finds out the weak places in his
very human body and soul. He is, too, and especially, a man of the
people with the native instincts of the scholar. The poetry of his
aspirations, the disinterestedness of his pursuit, the undyingness
of his passion, are made living to you, and some of the self-taught
man's vanity and his laboriousness of expression are not suppressed.
You think he must be cured for ever of his ambition that day when,
having received the 'terribly sensible' repulse from the head of
Bibliol College, he stood at the Crossway, and 'began to see that
the town life was a book of humanity infinitely more palpitating,
varied, and compendious than the gown life,' and at that supreme
moment when he, the obscure craftsman, wrote along the wall of
the dull college from whence the repulse had come, 'I have understanding as well as you.' But the passion is in his blood. He wanders
round and round the sacred places like a moth round a candle.
Christminster scenes mark the stages of his struggling, aspiring life.
The imaginative child, watching from the roof of the Brown House
the far-off spires and domes, the night-wandering stonemason
'under the walls and doorways, feeling with his fingers the con-
tours of their mouldings,' the ghosts of old scholars, comrades of his
solitude, are striking pictures out of his early, hopeful time. In his
sick and unfortunate days, when forced to labour at an earlier-
learnt trade than his own, he, as Arabella says, 'still harps on
Christminster, even in his cakes,' shaping these with grotesque

pathos to a reminiscence of traceried windows and cloisters. There, too, he dies, lonely and obscure, to the hum of a college chapel organ, and the shouts of Commemoration games. A poor workman to the end, a boyish imprudence for which he never shirked the payment, dogged him persistently; and the woman who had been his light and leader left him in the darkness, to fulfil, for superstition's sake, a loathed duty.

His career may wholesomely astonish some middle-class readers, inasmuch as it goes to prove that aspiring and sensitive souls do not need generations of literary education and genteel incomes to breed them; and that poverty and the stress of life reveal to such sensitive souls a world that the comfortably-placed and the unimaginative only deny because they have been saved and denied the chance of entrance.

Sue's story is a reality, with some unhappy exaggeration about it; but all that concerns Jude, in his strength and weakness, is masterly and written out of a deep heart. The constant lover—constant for all the Arabella incidents—makes, perhaps, widest appeal for sympathy. But it is another Jude on which Mr. Hardy has shed the full light of his imagination; and the wandering, rejected scholar flits a pathetic ghost through college gate-ways and by college walls for evermore.   A. M.

The Bookman (New York), January 1896
'A Novel of Lubricity'

... The characters of the book are Jude Fawley, a peasant by birth, who is possessed of an intense yearning which is never gratified, for scholarly distinction, and of refined and spiritual traits which exist side by side with a lurking love of sensuality and drink; one Arabella, a typical barmaid, coarse, brazen, and cunning; Jude's cousin Sue, an Anglicised version of one of Marcel Prévost's *demi-vierges;* and a certain village schoolmaster named Phillotson, who has some unexplained sexual peculiarities at which Mr. Hardy, for a wonder, only hints. Jude is tricked into an early marriage with Arabella, and Sue is forced into one with Phillotson. Both marriages are ended by divorce, whereupon Jude and his cousin live together in unlawful relations, until an accumulation of disasters converts Jude into a sceptic and Sue into an hysterical *dévote*, whereupon they separate, Sue remarrying her schoolmaster as a matter of conscience, and Jude remarrying Arabella as a matter of desperation.

Such, in brief, is an outline of the story, which, even as Mr.

Hardy tells it, is improbable, but which one would not criticise were it not for his extraordinary lack of reticence in the telling. There is nothing in the plot that justifies the grossness with which he has chosen to elaborate its details. Nor is this grossness the grossness of the English novelists of the last century—of Fielding and Smollett—with whom Mr. Hardy has many traits in common. It does not suggest the rude virility of young and lusty Englishmen, with huge calves and broad backs and vigorous health; of strapping fellows who roar out their broad jokes over a mug of ale in the tap-room of a country inn. It is rather the studied satyriasis of approaching senility, suggesting the morbidly curious imaginings of a masochist or some other form of sexual pervert. The eagerness with which every unclean situation is seized upon and carefully exploited recalls the spectacle of some foul animal that snatches greedily at great lumps of putrid offal which it mumbles with a hideous delight in the stenches that drive away all cleanlier creatures. We do not desire to dwell upon this subject. Our great objection to it is that it is wholly unnecessary, that in forcing us to batten upon such carrion, Mr. Hardy is sinning against light and wilfuly marring our appreciation of his grasp upon higher and nobler qualities than are the attributes of a scavenger.

. . . The fact is that Mr. Hardy tries to ride two horses—to be at one and the same time a romanticist and a realist, demanding for himself the romanticist's license in plot and the realist's license in incident. The result is a book that has none of the recognised claims to high literary rank; for it neither teaches a useful lesson, nor is it true to life. It is simply one of the most objectionable books that we have ever read in any language whatsoever.

. . . Some time ago we asked a distinguished critic what he thought of one of the younger of the French naturalistic novelists. 'Oh,' he said, carelessly, 'he is merely speculating in smut.' The expression is a crude one, and we should, perhaps, apologise for writing it down here; yet it serves our purpose excellently well, for in our judgment frankly and deliberately expressed, in *Jude the Obscure* Mr. Hardy is merely speculating in smut. *P.*

[? THE EDITOR, PROF. HARRY THURSTON PICK]

The Nation (New York), 6 February 1896

That hopefulness which perpetually affirms, even out of evil good must come, seldom meets with such immediate justification as in the clamor of disapproval raised against Mr. Hardy's novel 'Jude the Obscure.' He appears to have done a thing so repugnant to

modern English sentiment and taste that the extent of our supposed revolt against Puritanism may well be doubted—so far, at
least, as the word is a symbol for manners that correct and restrain
animal instincts, and for a decent reticence of speech. The tolera-
tion extended to inferior novelists who have for several years, under
various hypocritical pretexts, been engaged in the glorification of
sensuality, if not lust, may be ascribed, in view of this outburst of
wrath, partly to surprise at their audacity, and partly to a belief
that no permanent harm could be done by letting such very poor
players strut their little hour upon the stage and prance off into
secure oblivion. Mr. Hardy's 'Tess' made some people feel and say
that our literature was in danger of corruption. The vehement
denial by a serious and extremely competent novelist of some
principles upon which rests as successful a social system as poor
human nature has so far been able to evolve, was thought worth
consideration and rational protest. Still, there was but little frank
denunciation. The drama in 'Tess' was easily separable from the
argument, and made a direct appeal to passionate emotion well
adapted to confuse judgment, and even strong enough to win ad-
herents to the author's unequivocal expression of belief that, in the
question of society against Tess, society was flagrantly in the
wrong. In 'Jude' the author makes no special plea for the righteousness of conduct which long experience has qualified as depraved—
and, as a matter of fact, 'Jude,' judged by the strongest impression
made on the mind, is a less immoral book than 'Tess'; but it is
slightly coarser, many degrees colder; and therefore the average
intelligence, unclouded by emotion, perceives its offensiveness and
proclaims dissent.

Excepting pronounced hostility to marriage, whether regarded
as a Christian sacrament or a permanently binding legal contract,
the author's attitude towards the problems involved in his story is
as obscure as Jude. He is very bitter about matrimony. When Jude
and Arabella are swearing eternal fidelity before the parson, he
remarks: 'What was as remarkable as the undertaking itself was
the fact that nobody seemed at all surprised at what they swore.'
When Arabella makes a hideous scene, which there is no reason to
suppose she would not have made cheerfully and with great spirit
even if unmarried, Mr. Hardy thus interprets Jude's thoughts:
'Their lives were ruined; ruined by the fundamental error of their
matrimonial union—that of having based a permanent contract on
a temporary feeling which had no necessary connection with
affinities that alone render a life-long companionship tolerable.'
Again, when Arabella is parading her second victim at a fair, the

author's genial comment is, that 'they left the tent together in the antipathetic, recriminatory mood of the average husband and wife of Christendom.' Many more sentences might be quoted to show his fierce contempt for marriage, and we would believe that no more degrading condition could be imagined, were it not that he goes on to illustrate the pains and penalties of an illegal union and the madness of divorce. Therefore, he seems to stand as an advocate for celibacy and the extinction of the race. In this position we shall have no further occasion to worry about him; he may be permitted to cherish his convictions unenvied and undisturbed. . . .

The Saturday Review, 8 February 1896

It is doubtful, considering not only the greatness of the work but also the greatness of the author's reputation, whether for many years any book has received quite so foolish a reception as has been accorded the last and most splendid of all the books that Mr. Hardy has given the world. By an unfortunate coincidence it appears just at the culmination of a new fashion in Cant, the Cant of 'Healthiness.' It is now the better part of a year ago since the collapse of the 'New Woman' fiction began. The success of 'The Woman Who Did' was perhaps the last of a series of successes attained, in spite of glaring artistic defects, and an utter want of humour or beauty, by works dealing intimately and unrestrainedly with sexual affairs. It marked a crisis. A respectable public had for a year or more read such books eagerly, and discussed hitherto unheard of topics with burning ears and an air of liberality. The reviewers had reviewed in the spirit of public servants. But such strange delights lead speedily to remorse and reaction. The pendulum bob of the public conscience swung back swiftly and forcibly. From reading books wholly and solely dependent upon sexuality for their interest, the respectable public has got now to rejecting books wholly and solely for their recognition of sexuality, however incidental that recognition may be. And the reviewers, mindful of the fact that the duty of a reviewer is to provide acceptable reading for his editor's public, have changed with the greatest dexterity from a chorus praising 'outspoken purity' to a band of public informers against indecorum. It is as if the spirit of McDougallism has fled the London County Council to take refuge in the circles called 'literary.' So active, so malignant have these sanitary inspectors of fiction become, that a period of terror, analogous to that of the New England Witch Mania, is upon us. No novelist, however respectable, can deem himself altogether safe to-day from a charge of morbidity and unhealthiness. They spare neither age nor sex; the beginner of yesterday and the maker of a dozen respectable novels suffer alike. They outdo one another in their alertness for anything they can by any possible measure of language contrive to call *decadent*. One scarcely dares leave a man and woman together within the same corners for fear of their scandal; one dares scarcely whisper of reality. And at the very climax of this silliness, Mr. Hardy, with an admirable calm, has put forth a book in which a secondary, but very important, interest is a frank treatment of the destructive influence of a vein of sensuality upon an ambitious working-man. There probably never was a novel dealing with the closer relations of men and women that was quite so free from lasciviousness as this. But at one point a symbolical piece of offal is flung into Jude's face. Incontinently a number of popular reviewers, almost tumbling over one another in the haste to be first, have rushed into print under such headings as 'Jude the Obscene,' and denounced the book, with simply libellous violence, as a mass of filth from beginning to end.

If the reader has trusted the reviewers for his estimate of this great novel, he may even be surprised to learn that its main theme is not sexual at all; that the dominant motive of Jude's life is the fascination Christminster (Oxford) exercises upon his rustic imagination, and that the climax of its development is the pitiless irony of Jude's death-scene, within sound of the University he loved— which he loved, but which could offer no place in all its colleges for such a man as he. Only as a modifying cause does the man's sexuality come in, just as much as, and no more than, it comes into the life of any serious but healthy man. For the first time in English literature the almost intolerable difficulties that beset an ambitious man of the working class—the snares, the obstacles, the countless rejections and humiliations by which our society eludes the services of these volunteers—receive adequate treatment. And since the peculiar matrimonial difficulties of Jude's cousin Sue have been treated *ad nauseam* in the interests of purity in our contemporaries, we may perhaps give her but an incidental mention in this review, and devote ourselves to the neglected major theme of the novel. . . .

It is impossible by scrappy quotations to do justice to Mr. Hardy's tremendous indictment of the system which closes our three English teaching Universities to what is, and what has always been, the noblest material in the intellectual life of this country— the untaught. Sufficient has been quoted to show how entirely false is the impression that this book relies mainly upon its treatment of sex trouble—that it is to be regarded as a mere artistic and elaborate essay upon the great 'Woman Who' theme. That is really as much criticism as is needed here just now. The present reviewer will not even pretend to taste and dubitate, to advise and reprimand, in the case of a book that alone will make 1895 a memorable year in the history of literature. . . .

The Idler, February 1896

. . . Not all Mr. Hardy's strenuous 'purpose' in *Jude the Obscure* (Osgood, McIlvaine & Co.) can rob him of a novelist's first great gift, the power of creating living human beings. It is true that Jude and Sue have their lapses into unreality, and there are situations in the book which it takes all Mr. Hardy's dramatic power to make credible, but allowing to the full all such criticisms *Jude* remains perhaps the most powerful and moving picture of human life which Mr. Hardy has given us. No doubt the picture is dark, darker, perhaps, even than reality. Such pessimism is only half true of life as a whole. *Jude*, indeed, is a masterly piece of special pleading; much as was *Les Misérables*. But just as in optimistic novels of the old pattern, the hero is blessed with impossible good fortune from start to finish, Val Jean and Jude are cursed with almost equally bad luck. In one case everything prospers: in the other everything goes wrong. A malignant fate seems to dog their footsteps, at every turn of the way they make tragic mistakes, and their very wisdom is always for the worst. Undoubtedly there are actual lives of such unrelieved misfortune, and a novelist is quite within his right in taking such for his theme, yet he must not present them to us as typical human lives—for such, even amid the hardest conditions, they are not. Too many reviewers have treated *Jude* as a polemic against marriage. Nothing could be more unjust. It is true that the tragedy of Jude and Sue was partly brought about by the marriage laws, but their own weakness of character was mainly responsible for it; and Mr. Hardy's novel, in so far as it is an indictment, is an indictment of much older and crueller laws than those relating to marriage, the laws of the universe. It is a Promethean indictment of that power, which, in Omar's words,

> 'with pitfall and with gin,
> Beset the path we were to wander in,'

and to conceive it merely as a criticism of marriage is to miss its far more universal tragic significance. . . .

RICHARD LE GALLIENNE

The Yorkshire Post, 8 June 1896

(A letter to the editor from Bishop William Walsham How)

BISHOPGARTH, WAKEFIELD.

SIR,

Will you allow me to publicly thank you for your outspoken leader in your to-day's issue denouncing the intolerable grossness and hateful sneering at all that one most reveres in such writers as Thomas Hardy?

On the authority of one of those reviews which you justly condemn for this reticence, I bought a copy of one of Mr. Hardy's novels, but was so disgusted with its insolence and indecency that I threw it into the fire. It is a disgrace to our great public libraries to admit such garbage, clever though it may be, to their shelves.

I am, sir,

Yours, &c.,

WM. WALSHAM WAKEFIELD.

The Savoy, October 1896

. . . Your wholesome-minded novelist knows that the life of a pure-natured Englishwoman after marriage is, as Taine said, mainly that of a very broody hen, a series of merely physiological processes with which he, as a novelist, has no further concern.

But in novels, as in life, one comes at length to realize that marriage is not necessarily either a grave, or a convent gate, or a hen's nest, that though the conditions are changed the forces at work remain largely the same. It is still quite possible to watch the passions at play, though there may now be more tragedy or more pathos in the outcome of that play. This Mr. Hardy proceeded to do, first on a small scale in short stories, and then on a larger scale. . . .

I was not without suspicion in approaching 'Jude the Obscure.' Had Mr. Hardy discovered the pernicious truth that whereas children can only take their powders in jam, the strenuous British public cannot be induced to devour their jam unless convinced that it contains some strange and nauseous powder? Was 'Jude the Obscure' a sermon on marriage from the text on the title-page: 'The letter killeth'? Putting-aside the small failures always liable to occur in Mr. Hardy's work, I found little to justify the suspicion. The sermon may, possibly, be there, but the spirit of art has, at all events, not been killed. In all the great qualities of literature 'Jude the Obscure' seems to me the greatest novel written in England for many years.

It is interesting to compare 'Jude' with a characteristic novel of Mr. Hardy's earlier period, with 'A pair of Blue Eyes,' or 'The Return of the Native.' On going back to these, after reading 'Jude,' one notes the graver and deeper tones in the later book, the more austere and restrained roads of art which Mr. Hardy has sought to follow, and the more organic and radical way in which he now grips the individuality of his creatures. The individuals themselves have not fundamentally changed. The type of womankind that Mr. Hardy chiefly loves to study, from Cytherea to Sue, has always been the same, very human, also very feminine, rarely with any marked element of virility, and so contrasting curiously with the androgynous heroines loved of Mr. Meredith. The latter, with their resolute daring and energy, are of finer calibre and more imposing; they are also very much rarer in the actual world than Mr. Hardy's women, who represent, it seems to me, a type not uncommon in the south of England, where the heavier Teutonic and Scandinavian elements are, more than elsewhere, modified by the alert and volatile elements furnished by earlier races. But if the type remains the same the grasp of it is now much more thorough. At first Mr. Hardy took these women chiefly at their more obviously charming or pathetic moments, and sought to make the most of those moments, a little careless as to the organic connection of such moments to the underlying personality. One can well understand that many readers should prefer the romantic charm of the earlier passages, but—should it be necessary to affirm?—to grapple with complexly realized persons and to dare to face them in the tragic or sordid crises of real life is to rise to a higher plane of art. In 'Jude the Obscure' there is a fine self-restraint, a complete mastery of all the elements of an exceedingly human story. There is nothing here of the distressing melodrama into which Mr. Hardy was wont to fall in his early novels. Yet in plot 'Jude' might be a farce. One could imagine that Mr. Hardy had purposed to himself to take a conventional farce, in which a man and a woman leave their respective partners to make love to one another and then finally rejoin their original partners, in order to see what could be made of such a story by an artist whose sensitive vision penetrated to the tragic irony of things; just as the great novelists of old, De la Sale, Cervantes, Fielding, took the worn-out conventional stories of their time, and filled them with the immortal blood of life. Thus 'Jude' has a certain symmetry of plan such as is rare in the actual world—where we do not so readily respond to our cues—but to use such a plot to produce such an effect is an achievement of the first order. . . .

But I understand that the charge brought against 'Jude the Obscure' is not so much that it is bad art as that it is a book with a purpose, a moral or an immoral purpose, according to the standpoint of the critic. It would not be pleasant to admit that a book you thought bad morality is good art, but the bad morality is the main point, and this book, it is said, is immoral, and indecent as well.

So are most of our great novels. . . .

. . . It seems, indeed, on a review of all the facts, that the surer a novel is of a certain immortality, the surer it is also to be regarded at first as indecent, as subversive of public morality. So that when, as in the present case, such charges are recklessly flung about in all the most influential quarters, we are simply called upon to accept them placidly as necessary incidents in the career of a great novel.

It is no fortuitous circumstance that the greatest achievements of the novelist's art seem to outrage morality. 'Jude the Obscure' is a sufficiently great book to serve to illustrate a first principle. I have remarked that I cannot find any undue intrusion of morality in the art of this book. But I was careful to express myself cautiously, for without doubt the greatest issues of social morality are throughout at stake. So that the question arises: What is the function of the novelist as regards morals? The answer is simple, though it has sometimes been muddled. A few persons have incautiously asserted that the novel has nothing to do with morals. That we cannot assert; the utmost that can be asserted is that the novelist should never allow himself to be made the tool of a merely moral or immoral purpose. For the fact is that, so far as the moralist deals with life at all, morals is part of the very stuff of his art. That is to say, that his art lies in drawing the sinuous woof of human nature between the rigid warp of morals. Take away morals, and the novelist is *in vacuo*, in the region of fairy land. The more subtly and firmly he can weave these elements together the more impressive becomes the stuff of his art. The great poet may be in love with passion, but it is by heightening and strengthening the dignity of traditional moral law that he gives passion fullest play. When Wagner desired to create a typically complete picture of passion he chose the story of Tristram; no story of Paul and Virginia can ever bring out the deepest cries of human passion. Shakespeare found it impossible to picture even the pure young love of Romeo and Juliet without the aid of the violated laws of family and tradition. 'The crash of broken commandments,' Mr. Hardy once wrote in a magazine article, 'is as necessary an accompaniment to the catastrophe of a tragedy as the noise of drum and cymbals to a triumphal march;' and that picturesque image fails to express how essential to the dramatist is this clash of law against passion. It is the same in life as in art, and if you think of the most pathetic stories of human passion, the profoundest utterances of human love, you probably think most readily of such things as the letters of Abélard and Héloise, or of Mlle. de Lespinasse, or of the Portuguese nun, and only with difficulty of the tamer speech of happier and more legitimate emotions. Life finds her game in playing off the irresistible energy of the individual against the equally irresistible energy of the race, and the stronger each is the finer the game. So the great artist whose brain is afire with the love of passion yet magnifies the terror and force of moral law, in his heart probably hates it.

Mr. Hardy has always been in love with Nature, with the instinctive, spontaneous, unregarded aspects of Nature, from the music of the dead heatherbells to the flutter of tremulous human hearts, all the things that are beautiful because they are uncontrolled by artificial constraint. The progress of his art has consisted in bringing this element of nature into ever closer contact with the rigid routine of life, making it more human, making it more moral or more immoral. It is an inevitable progression. That love of the spontaneous, the primitive, the unbound—which we call the love of 'Nature'—must as it becomes more searching take more and more into account those things, also natural, which bind and constrain 'Nature.' So that on the one side, as Mr. Hardy has himself expressed it, we have Nature and her unconsciousness of all but essential law, on the other the laws framed merely as social expedients without a basis in the heart of things, and merely expressing the triumph of the majority over the individual; which shows, as is indeed evident from Mr. Hardy's work, that he is not much in sympathy with Society, and also shows that, like Heyse, he recognizes a moral order in Nature. This conflict reaches its highest point around women. Truly or falsely, for good or for evil, woman has always been for man the supreme priestess, or the supreme devil, of Nature. 'A woman,' said Proudhon—himself the incarnation of the revolt of Nature in the heart of man—'even the most charming and virtuous woman, always contains an element of cunning, the wild beast element. She is a tamed animal that sometimes returns to her natural instinct. This cannot be said in the same degree of man.' The loving student of the elemental in Nature so becomes the loving student of women, the sensitive historian of her conflicts with 'sin' and with 'repentance,' the creations of man. Not, indeed, that any woman who has 'sinned,' if her sin was indeed love, ever really 'repents.' It is probable that a true experience of the one emotional state as of the other remains a little foreign to her, 'sin' having probably been the invention of men who never really knew what love is. She may catch the phrases of the people around her when her spirit is broken, but that is all. I have never known or heard of any woman, having for one moment in her life loved and been loved, who did not count that moment as worth all other moments in life. The consciousness of the world's professed esteem can never give to unloved virtue and respectability the pride which belongs to the woman who has once 'sinned' with all her heart. One supposes that the slaves of old who never once failed in abject obedience to their master's will mostly subdued their souls to the level of their starved virtues. But the woman who has loved is like the slave who once at least in his life has risen in rebellion with the cry: 'And I, too, am a man!' Nothing that comes after can undo the fine satisfaction of that moment. It was so that a great seventeenth-century predecessor of Mr. Hardy in the knowledge of the heart, painted Annabella exultant in her sin even at the moment of discovery, for 'Nature' knows no sin.

If these things are so, it is clear how the artist who has trained himself to the finest observation of Nature cannot fail, as his art becomes more vital and profound, to paint morals. The fresher and more intimate his vision of Nature, the more startling his picture of morals. To such an extent is this the case in 'Jude the Obscure,' that some people have preferred to regard the book as a study of monstrosity, of disease. Sue is neurotic, some critics say; it is fashionable to play cheerfully with terrible words you know nothing about. 'Neurotic' these good people say by way of dismissing her, innocently unaware that many a charming 'urban miss' of their own acquaintance would deserve the name at least as well. In representing Jude and Sue as belonging to a failing family stock, I take it that Mr. Hardy by no means wished to bring before us a mere monstrosity, a pathological 'case,' but that rather, with an artist's true instinct—the same instinct that moved so great an artist as Shakespeare when he conceived 'Hamlet'—he indicates the channels of least resistance along which the forces of life most impetuously rush. Jude and Sue are represented as crushed by a civilization to which they were not born, and though civilization may in some respects be regarded as a disease and as unnatural, in others it may be said to bring out those finer vibrations of Nature which are overlaid by rough and bucolic conditions of life. The refinement of sexual sensibility with which this book largely deals is precisely such a vibration. To treat Jude, who wavers between two women, and Sue, who finds the laws of marriage too mighty for her lightly-poised organism, as shocking monstrosities, reveals a curious attitude in the critics who have committed themselves to that view. Clearly they consider human sexual relationships to be as simple as those of the farmyard. They are as shocked as a farmer would be to find that a hen had views of her own concerning the lord of the harem. If, let us say, you decide that Indian Game and Plymouth Rock make a good cross, you put your cock and hens together, and the matter is settled; and if you decide that a man and a woman are in love with each other, you marry them and the matter is likewise settled for the whole term of their natural lives. I suppose that the farmyard view really is the view of the ordinary wholesome-minded novelist—I mean of course in England—and of his ordinary critic. Indeed in Europe generally, a distinguished German anthropologist has lately declared, sensible and experienced men still often exhibit a knowledge of sexual matters such as we might expect from a milkmaid. But assuredly the farmyard view corresponds imperfectly to the facts of human life in our time. Such things as 'Jude' is made of are, in our time at all events, life, and life is still worthy of her muse. . . .

To sum up, 'Jude the Obscure' seems to me—in such a matter one can only give one's own impressions for what they are worth—a singularly fine piece of art, when we remember the present position of the English novel. It is the natural outcome of Mr. Hardy's development, along lines that are genuinely and completely English. It deals very subtly and sensitively with new and modern aspects of life, and if, in so doing, it may be said to represent Nature as often cruel to our social laws, we must remark that the strife of Nature and Society, the individual and the community, has ever been the artist's opportunity. 'Matrimony have growed to be that serious in these days,' Widow Edlin remarks, 'that one really do feel afeard to move in it at all.' It is an affectation to pretend that the farmyard theory of life still rules unquestioned, and that there are no facts to justify Mrs. Edlin. If anyone will not hear her, let him turn to the Registrar-General. Such facts are in our civilisation to-day. We have no right to resent the grave and serious spirit with which Mr. Hardy, in the maturity of his genius, has devoted his best art to picture some of these facts. In 'Jude the Obscure' we find for the first time in our literature the reality of marriage clearly recognized as something wholly apart from the mere ceremony with which our novelists have usually identified it.

Others among our novelists may have tried to deal with the reality rather than with its shadow, but assuredly not with the audacity, purity and sincerity of an artist who is akin in spirit to the great artists of our best dramatic age, to Fletcher and Heywood and Ford, rather than to the powerful though often clumsy novelists of the eighteenth century.

There is one other complaint often brought against this book, I understand, by critics usually regarded as intelligent, and with the mention of it I have done. 'Mr. Hardy finds that marriage often leads to tragedy,' they say, 'but he shows us no way out of these difficulties; he does not tell us his own plans for the improvement of marriage and the promotion of morality.' Let us try to consider this complaint with due solemnity. It is true that the artist is god in his own world; but being so he has too fine a sense of the etiquette of creation to presume to offer suggestions to the creator of the actual world, suggestions which might be resented, and would almost certainly not be adopted. An artist's private opinions concerning the things that are good and bad in the larger world are sufficiently implicit in the structure of his own smaller world; the counsel that he should make them explicit in a code of rules and regulations for humanity at large is a counsel which, as every artist knows, can only come from the Evil One. This complaint against 'Jude the Obscure' could not have arisen save among a generation which has battened on moral and immoral tracts thrown into the form of fiction by ingenious novices. The only cure for it one can suggest is a course of great European novels from 'Petit Jehan de Saintré' downwards. One suggestion indeed occurs for such consolation as it may yield. Has it not been left to our century to discover that the same hand which wrote the disordered philosophy of 'Hamlet' put the times into joint again in 'The New Atlantis,' and may not posterity find Thomas Hardy's hand in 'Looking Backward' and 'The Strike of a Sex?' Thus for these critics of 'Jude' there may yet be balm in Utopia.   HAVELOCK ELLIS

The Quarterly Review, April 1904

From 'The Novels of Thomas Hardy'

... 'Jude the Obscure,' that much discussed work, is another of Mr. Hardy's essays in metaphysics. It is a wild attempt to realise in narrative form some current pessimistic theories, by imagining a world where all women will have an innate aversion against marrying and bearing children; and where, even when children are born, they will resort to suicide out of an instinctive desire not to live. These ideas are embodied in Sue Bridehead, and the son of Jude. Mr Hardy would have us believe that Jude Fawley came from Mellstock where lived that more amiable idiot Tommy Leaf, and the gallant Dick Dewy. As a matter of fact, Jude is a native of that part of the Utopia of the philosophers over which the author of 'The Metaphysics of Love' dismally reigns. He is Schopenhauer's perfidious lover 'seeking to perpetuate all this misery and turmoil which otherwise would come to a timely end.' Lest the shade of the great hypochondriac should thereby be offended, Jude is also intended to personify the more gratifying idea of the rapid extinction of the human race by degeneration. Some very unpleasant details are introduced in order to make the account of this ghastly hallucination resemble a novel of misery, but vainly; the principal characters and the main events, as described, are as far removed from the realities of this world as are those in the 'Well-beloved.' What is but too real and apparent is the frame of mind of which the work is an expression. One sees that the professed humanitarian in our day can excel Swift himself in appalling misanthropy.

Besides revealing Mr Hardy's impressions of his fellow-creatures and the universe generally, 'Jude the Obscure' is significant in regard to his relation to contemporary thought. The author represents the younger and more febrile generation who inherited the ideas of the rationalists by whom George Eliot was disciplined in thought. The world, in their view, was not under divine governance; men, instead of being immortal souls, were mere animals, which would at last yield up their place on earth to some lower type better fitted to survive in more degrading conditions; in the meantime, they said, let us promote righteousness and do our best to make the lot of the survivors of our race as pleasant as possible. From their peculiar standpoint they were illogical but human; Mr Hardy is inhuman but logical. They denied the evidence of the religious instincts because these were something that could not be measured by the utilitarian standard of immediate pleasure and immediate pain; he applied the same test of rationalistic enquiry to the ethical code to which George Eliot, for example, had adhered amid all her doubts. 'Jude the Obscure' is his answer to his teachers. He replies, in effect, that since, as you say, the travail of the whole human race, of the whole world, leads in the end to nothing, duty, morality, and life itself to me are nothing: 'What is it all but a trouble of ants?' as Tennyson said, speculating on the same idea only to reject it vehemently.

10

> 'Then bitter self-reproaches as I stood
> I dealt me silently,
> As one perverse—misrepresenting Good,
> In graceless mutiny.'

So Mr Hardy writes in one of his poems. And in this passage he shows, at least, that, despite the inordinate power which a sensibility so quick, delicate, and acute as not to be entirely healthy, exerts over his imagination, he can at times perceive something else than a soul of evil in things that the rest of men account to be good. Yet we must admit that, even from the verses in question, it is evident how completely his judgment is swayed by feeling, for it was only in the æsthetic rapture of gazing at a lean black stretch of moorland, transfigured in the light of a setting sun, that he was moved to accuse himself so sternly. . . .

EDWARD WRIGHT

¶ In *The New Review* for January 1890 Hardy published an essay on 'Candour in English Fiction', in which he lamented the 'wellnigh insuperable bar' which English society imposed on the treatment of the sexual relationship as it is. Any attempt to go beyond 'the regulation finish that "they married and were happy ever after"' was made impossible by the novel-reading public who, though they might desire true views for their own reading, 'insist, for a plausible but questionable reason, upon false views for the reading of young people'. The result is the exclusion from current literature of the stuff from which most of the world's masterpieces have been made.

> The crash of broken commandments is as necessary an accompaniment to the catastrophe of a tragedy as the noise of drum and cymbals to a triumphant march. But the crash of broken commandments shall not be heard; or, if at all, but gently, like the roaring of Bottom—gently as any sucking dove, or as 'twere any nightingale, lest we should fright the ladies out of their wits.

This is the article which Havelock Ellis refers to in his review in *The Savoy*. 'The surer a novel is of a certain immortality, the surer it is also to be regarded at first as indecent, as subversive of public morality': Ellis clearly agreed with Hardy, and realised that *Jude* was an excellent illustration of the point. The outcry that the book produced is well known, and Hardy himself later claimed that the experience completely cured him of further interest in novel-writing. We can never know, of course, if this is true: such theories grow easily, and even when they are put out by the writer himself, we may wonder if he too is the easy victim of a lust for legend. There is a fragment of evidence—not as well known as the remark of Hardy's mentioned above—to suggest that his reasons for giving up novel-writing were more complex and deep-seated. In a little book called *Thomas Hardy at Max Gate* (1928), Vere H. Collins describes a number of interviews with Hardy, during one of which they had this exchange:

'Mr. Hardy, if it is not asking too intimate a question, may I know whether there is any truth in the rumour that certain attacks in the press made on *Jude* decided you not to write any more novels?'

Hardy (shortly): 'Not just what the papers said. I never cared very much about writing novels. And I should not have— (pause). Besides, I had written quite enough novels. Some people go on writing so many that they cannot remember their titles . . .'

The reception of *Jude* was not, in fact, as simply hostile as legend says. It is true there were some savage attacks, but there were also a few enthusiastic defences. The picture is not very different from the mixed reception that greeted *Tess*: though there was, to be sure, a new note of vituperation, to be seen even in the titles of the reviews ('Jude the Obscene', 'Hardy the Degenerate', 'A Novel of Lubricity', etc.).

A series of angry denunciations grows tedious; but it seemed to us necessary to include several of the attacks on the novel, in order to show their frequency and their variety of tone. The most famous was perhaps the *Pall Mall Gazette*'s 'Jude the Obscene', and this we have given in full, together with the pained disapproval of *The Guardian*, a paragraph from the violent sarcasm of *The World*, and the splendid clerical denunciation of Bishop How. The most ambitious attack was Mrs Oliphant's, in *Blackwood's*. Her purpose, she explains, is not that of criticism; she is writing to ask whether the success of *Jude*, and a novel by Grant Allen, means that ordinary people want to see marriage attacked, and free sexual union advocated. The article begins with a lament that English novels are, in one respect, still more scandalous than French.

> For in France the pure woman is still a being to be surrounded with every reverence and respect—whereas in the last new development of English fiction, that character has undergone a complete and extraordinary transformation, and it is the indulgence of passion, not the restraint of it, which is considered to be specially characteristic of purity.

This seems to bear out the *Saturday Review*'s suggestion, that the attack on *Jude* was partly a reaction against the Cant of Healthiness. We have given a bit of this opening lament, and most of the discussion of *Jude*, omitting the plot summary and the ridicule of the hanging episode: 'Mr Hardy knows, no doubt as everybody does, that the children are a most serious part of the question of the abolition of marriage. Is this the way in which he considers it would be resolved best?'

Hardy pasted this review in his scrap-book, and added a comment: 'The foregoing article is by Mrs Oliphant who had novels of her own to sell to magazines.'

The English reviewers were mild compared to the Americans. 'Will these realists leave nothing to the imagination?' fumed the Chicago *Dial*. No English reviewer equalled the savagery of the New York *Bookman*: '. . . some foul animal that snatches greedily at great lumps of putrid offal which it mumbles with a hideous delight in the stenches that drive away all cleanlier creatures.' This fact is so striking that is has tempted us, against our general rule, to include a good sample of American notices.

We know something of Hardy's reaction to one of the American reviews, that by Jeannette L. Gilder in the New York *World*. After reading it he wrote to Harper:

> I am much surprised, and I may say distressed, by the nature of the attack . . . in the New York *World*. . . . It is so much against my wish to offend the tastes of the American public, or to thrust any book of mine upon readers there, that if it should be in your own judgment advisable, please withdraw the novel.

Harper's Weekly had already printed the page quoted on p. 104 and the novel was not, of course, withdrawn. There is an epilogue to this story. The following summer Miss Gilder was in London, and wrote to Hardy asking for an interview.

I hear that you want to brain me with Sitting Bull's war club. Instead of that, pour coals of fire on my head by letting me interview you regarding *Jude*. I should like to get your side of the argument. . . .

Hardy's very characteristic reply is given in Florence Emily Hardy's *Life*. He refused to see her, because he had refused to be interviewed by anyone about *Jude* 'and you must make allowance for human nature when I tell you that I do not feel disposed to depart from this rule in favour of the author of the review of the novel in the *New York World*'. As for her wish to publish his 'side of the argument', he says, with his oddly sincere self-deprecation, 'The rectification of judgements, etc., and the way in which my books are interpreted, do not much interest me.' Hardy's natural kindliness came out in a final paragraph expressing his pleasure at her 'kindly wish to set right any misapprehension you may have caused'. Miss Gilder replied to this in one sentence: 'I knew you were a great man, but I did not appreciate your goodness until I received your letter this morning.'

America produced one of the most intelligent defences of the book, that by the novelist William Dean Howells in *Harper's Weekly*: Howells had met Hardy in London in 1883, had then started to read his novels (beginning with *A Pair of Blue Eyes*!), and had reviewed *The Mayor of Casterbridge* favourably in *Harper's Magazine*. He and Hardy respected each other highly, and Howells placed Hardy among the 'authors I must call my masters'. America produced, too, one hostile notice whose sarcasms should not blind us to its intelligence. The critic of *The Nation* found in the book a 'fierce contempt for marriage': like Mrs Oliphant, he was less concerned with literary criticism than with the didactic implications of the novel. They both underrate or ignore the book's power, yet who can blame the critic for being didactic when the author was didactic first? *Jude is* an attack on marriage; and some years later Hardy published an article on the marriage laws (*Hearst's Magazine*, June 1912), which makes it clear that his attack is a radical one, and in which he says explicitly that he is repeating points he has made many times during the past twenty or thirty years.

As the English marriage laws are, to the eyes of anybody who looks around, the gratuitous cause of at least half the misery of the community, that they are allowed to remain in force for a day is, to quote the famous last word of the ceremony itself, an 'amazement', and can only be accounted for by the assumption that we live in a barbarous age, and are the slaves of gross superstition.

When it comes to the question of what is to be done Hardy is modest ('it is rather a question for experts than for me'), and then suggests something not very different from what we have now:

I can only suppose, in a general way, that a marriage should be dissolvable on the wish of either party, if that party can prove a cruelty to him or her, provided (probably) that the maintenance of the children (if any) should be borne by the breadwinner.

The contrasting tone of these two paragraphs surely makes it clear that he was much more deeply concerned in his attack than in suggestions for remedies; and since the indignation of Mrs Oliphant and the sarcasms of *The Nation* say just this, we ought not to dismiss them too contemptuously.

'Sue is altogether a strange and unnatural creature,' said *The Morning Post*. She is the strangest of all Hardy's creations, and one of the most haunting: his version of the new woman. Yet there is one thing about her that is puzzling, and that ought—surely—to be cleared up. What was wrong in Sue's marriage? Hardy is praised—or blamed—for the outspokenness with which he showed her physical repugnance: the scene in which Phillotson blunders into their bedroom and she jumps out of the window in terror is one of those in which Hardy, verging on the ludicrous, remains oddly moving. But the novelist who begins to be outspoken must not stop half-way: and the result of Hardy's 'lubricity' is to leave us less satisfied than a more reticent novelist would have left us, for he raises questions that he does not answer. In particular, he raises the question, Did Sue hate Phillotson, or did she hate sex? Is

Hardy portraying the sufferings of a woman who has found herself with a physically incompatible mate, or a frigid woman? The
difference is surely important; and it implies the further question,
what were her sexual relations with Jude like?

The novel as we have it suggests that Hardy did not make up his
mind on this: though his letter to Edmund Gosse (above) seems to
make it clear that he would have liked to indicate that Sue was
frigid, but was afraid to be so outspoken. The reviewers are (of
course) even more reticent than the author, and it is impossible to
know how most of them took this point. Three of them, however,
do tell us something. *The Illustrated London News* says: 'Sue,
however, marries Phillotson, the schoolmaster, and finding that
match insupportable, rejoins Jude with her husband's consent.'
Does that imply that it was simply the match with Phillotson that
she found insupportable? Perhaps the critic is being too vague for
us to press his meaning: but the remaining two are more definite.
The Bookman (New York), which speaks of 'a certain village
schoolmaster named Phillotson, who has some unexplained sexual
peculiarities at which Mr Hardy, for a wonder, only hints', is certainly assuming that the aversion was to Phillotson only; on the
other hand, the female critic of the London *Bookman* says of Sue,
'She could love and was not well fitted for marriage life. There she
is not so very abnormal. . . .' That the only two critics who are at
all definite on the point take opposite views seems clear enough
evidence of the ambiguity of what Hardy wrote.

Since critics had long been calling Hardy 'very French' and
comparing him to Zola, it may be worth while to add a French
opinion on him. To find this we must go a little beyond our chrono-
logical limit, to an article by Firmin Roz in *La Revue des Deux
Mondes* for 1 July 1906. M. Roz finds Hardy thoroughly English.
From the attacks on contemporary society in *Tess* and *Jude*, as
from the idyllic picture of unspoilt nature in the earlier novels, we
might conclude Hardy to be 'un Rousseau moins lyrique et tout
aussi ardent'. But this would be to misunderstand the essence of
his inspiration. For Hardy, M. Roz claims (and this is what makes
him so typically English), sees passion as a destructive force. He
is no romantic, but 'il voit la passion sans auréole, dans sa réalité
frémissante et douloureuse'.

An article in the same periodical which does not even mention
Hardy throws a certain light on the setting from which *Jude*

emerged. In the issue for 15 July 1895 there appeared, in the section on English affairs, a piece by T. de Wyzewa called 'la Femme nouvelle'. Part of it is about novels: 'Le nouveau roman anglais diffère surtout de l'ancien en ce qu'il est *sexualiste*. . . . Ce que les Anglais appellent la littérature sexualiste correspond assez exactement a ce qu'a été naguère chez nous le naturalisme.' Such a change in English habits brings one sad consequence for the French: 'Ce n'est plus en Angleterre désormais que les mères françaises pourront s'approvisionner, en toute confiance, de romans pour leurs filles.' In July 1895 *Jude* was still in the press, and though some of the instalments would by then have appeared in America, it seems very unlikely that de Wyzewa could have seen them. Yet parts of his article sound like a description of it, and we must therefore conclude that it was less of a bombshell than some critics claimed. De Wyzewa's account of the strength of feminism and the 'roman sexualiste' is clearly describing the same phenomenon that the *Saturday Review* called the Cant of Healthiness, though he does not share the belief that it is over. Like M. Roz he does not believe that the English novelists are quite like the French; they are 'd'acharnés moralistes', 'chacun de leurs romans est le développement d'une thèse'. Unfortunately there is no record of whether de Wyzewa thought *Jude* an exception to this.

9 · GENERAL APPRAISALS

The Saturday Review, 4 January 1879

The question is perpetually suggesting itself nowadays whether it is better for a novel-writer to be clever or entertaining. Personally we have no doubt on the matter, but then the feelings of even a professional critic are apt to get the better of his principles. Possibly, in the interests of the highest art, we ought to hold up to the discriminating admiration of our readers the talent which we are compelled to recognize, although it has impressed more than delighted us. But we fear that if we took that sublime view of our vocation we should fail to carry our readers along with us; and, on the whole, it may be more advisable to be absolutely frank and speak out all we have upon our minds. We may appreciate the depth and brilliancy of George Eliot's later writings; but somehow we cannot fall into the same kindly and familiar companionship with *Middlemarch* and *Daniel Deronda* as with *Adam Bede* or the *Mill on the Floss;* and there is a rising school of novelists, of which Mr. Hardy is one of the ablest members, who seem to construct their fictions for themselves rather than for other people. It would be scarcely fair to say that they are dull; and they give us the fullest persuasion of a latent power which would enable them, as our ideas go, to write infinitely more agreeably if it pleased them. In one respect they resemble those fashionable and self-opinionated artists who embody their personal conceptions of art in forms that scandalize traditional opinions. In another respect, as we are glad to think, they differ from them very widely. For, whatever may be our estimate of their manner in the main, there is no denying the care they bestow upon their workmanship, and this is a thing to be grateful for in these days of slovenly writing. After all, however, we are brought round again to the point we started from. We maintain that the primary object of a story is to amuse, and in the attempt to amuse us Mr. Hardy, in our opinion, breaks down. In his case it has not been always so; but he would seem to be steadily subordinating interest to the rules by which he regulates his art. His *Under the Greenwood Tree* and *Pair of Blue Eyes*, partly perhaps because of rather unpromising names, were books that received less attention than they deserved. But his *Far from the Madding Crowd* was launched under favourable circumstances in a leading magazine, and—with reason—it won him a host of admirers. There may have been too much of the recurrence of marked mannerisms in it, with a good deal of what was hardly to be distinguished from affectation. But its characters were made living and breathing realities; there was a powerful love tale ingeniously worked out; the author showed a most intimate knowledge of the rural scenes he sympathetically described; and, above all, as is almost invariably his habit, he was quaintly humorous in the talk which he put into the mouths of his rustics. In this *Return of the Native* he has been less happy. The faults of *Far from the Madding Crowd* are exaggerated, and in the rugged and studied simplicity of its subject the story strikes us as intensely artificial. . . .

Letters to Living Authors, by John A. Steuart, 1890

. . . I have spoken at some length of Henchard, and called him one of your best creations, but he is not, by a long way, your only good one. Gabriel Oak, and a score or two others, might be named in the same sentence. And for general excellence it seems to me that you are almost, if not quite, unmatched among contemporary novelists. Such a book as *The Woodlanders* is enough to make one feel proud of one's generation, and, while it is always hard to predict what will live and what will not, I think it might surely be prophesied that that book will be known long after your generation. So, also, one would be inclined to say, will *Far from the Madding Crowd*, though not without a touch of melodrama here and there that is hardly in your best style; while, if fidelity and idealism count for anything, *Under the Greenwood Tree* is as sure of life as anything that has been done in our day.

I understand you are no favourite with the young lady who patronises the circulating libraries. She is in the habit of making marginal notes in your books which are sometimes more entertaining than complimentary. Precisely why the fair one quarrels with you is, of course, among the mysteries of the world, but it is vaguely understood she considers herself slandered in your female characters, so she calls you 'that horrid man Hardy,' a description which I suppose, to the feminine mind, expresses the height of disgust. What would she have? Mr. Lang, in upholding Thackeray in the face of detraction on the score of his female characters, says that people should really find fault with nature, and not with the novelist who copies nature. You might make a similar reply to your feminine critics. So long as Bathshebas are tolerably common in life, why should they not have their portraits painted? Your women are not conventional. They are not of the flaccid, pink and white type; but neither, so far as I can remember, are they inherently wicked. Let us have living creations—that is the great want in fiction—and that you give us in your women as well as in your men. Let us be thankful.

For power in describing scenery and natural objects generally, I hardly know your superior among novelists since Scott. Nay, I think that, in some respects, you are above the master himself. If he had the freer hand, you have, perhaps, the truer. Everywhere you are just as poetic as he, and generally far more minute—without being in the least tedious. There are as choice bits of description in your books as are to be met with in all fiction—I had almost said in all literature. In reading you, one often witnesses a whole world bursting into bloom; we feel the fragrance in our nostrils, and all but see the circulation of the sap in those woods you so much delight to describe. We have writers who are more fastidious about having nature always in holiday attire, but none who paints her more truthfully or feelingly as she is ordinarily, nor is there anything in the least sentimental in your love of nature. Rousseau has not infected you with his weakness, and you have not copied the lackadaisical whinings of so many of his disciples. In a word, in describing nature, as in all else you do, you are strong, and not only strong, but delightful. . . .

The Pall Mall Gazette, 2 January 1892
'Hodge' As I Know Him.
A Talk with Mr. Thomas Hardy

The ridge of a noble down, dark outlined against a pale green sky; a small red house standing in its own grounds close to the ancient town of Casterbridge—I mean Dorchester; a little drawing-room, the windows of which are flaming in the rays of the dying sun, and in which are seated two persons, Mr. Thomas Hardy, the novelist, the exponent, the exploiter, I might say, of the agricultural labourer, and myself, a quondam country parson—the representative on this occasion of the *Pall Mall Gazette*. Two people, therefore, very fairly capable of discussing Hodge and his peculiarities, though Mr. Hardy repeatedly assured me that he was himself no authority whatsoever on the subject:—

'All that I know about our Dorset labourers I gathered,' he said, 'from living in the country as a child and from thoroughly knowing their dialect. You cannot get at the labourer otherwise. Dialect is the only pass-key to anything like intimacy. I would not preserve dialect in its entirety, but I would extract from each dialect those words that have no equivalent in standard English and then use them; they would be most valuable, and our language would be greatly enriched thereby. Dialect is sadly dying out, and children down here in Dorset often have to ask their parents the meaning of a word. Conversation, therefore, is in quite a transition stage now in these parts. For instance, a funnel here used to be known as a tunniger; our servants in confusion coined the word "tunnel."'

Here a pause, while Mr. Hardy 'trigged' a shaky table.

'And now, Mr. Hardy,' said I, 'how do you explain the deadly dulness of village life?'—'In these parts,' he replied, 'to the fact that the "liviers"—people who held small copyholds for generations—are dying out. These people were not labourers, but small mechanics, little shopkeepers, who were the centre of village life. Nowadays people are all weekly tenants of the landlord, who take no interest in the place, who are not self-centred in any possible respect. Great credit is due to the parson, who, in my opinion, does much to keep up interest in these quiet villages. It would be a thousand pities that such men, educated, sympathetic, original-minded as many of them are, should be banished by looming difficulties of dogma, and the villages given over to the narrow-mindedness and lack of charity of some lower class of teacher.'

'How then do you explain the great dislike that exists in the rural breast for the parson?'—'I think he is so disliked, where he is disliked, more on account of his friendship with the squire and the powers that be; because he teaches a theology which they cannot square with the facts of life. The Liberationist Society are on the wrong tack; let them liberate the parson from his theology, not the parish from the parson.'

'But do you not think, Mr. Hardy, that on the whole the condition of the labourer is improving?'—'Emphatically, the young labourer is as happy as any man—the happiest in the community, indeed. It is complained that they are improvident, but, as a man once cynically remarked to me, "What is the good of our saving; we should never save as much as the parish would allow us?" The labouring classes are being raised by education to a marvellous extent.

'It is a curious fact, however,' continued Mr. Hardy, 'that the workmen are not so able-bodied as they were before education was as general as it now is. At present education is inclined to make them discontented; they are in a transition stage.'

'Do you believe in them as a coming force in politics?'—'They must be, by force of numbers, quantity rather than quality, I fear, at present. With most of them it is a matter of groping in the dark, of feeling rather than principle. They meet with a man they can trust on one subject and they understand him; they will trust him in all things, delivering over their political consciences into his keeping. They are getting much more worldly-wise, hereabouts at all events. They migrate every year, go from village to village, revelling in the change of scene and companionship. This opens their minds and understandings. Their women are singularly chaste —chaste, that is, in the sense that they are not wantonly inclined. As a rule, they do not drink to excess either. Their great dissipation here consists in the Saturday night's jaunt to the county or market town.

'These village councils of which they talk will be grand engines in the way of restoring the centrality of the old English village life. The men already talk of them with interest. It will be a great point gained, too, if the squires and landholders will let people have little freeholds. It would be greatly to the interest of the squirearchy. They would gain many allies. A man would give anything for half an acre. "No," says my Lord the Squire. He makes an enemy, whilst by a kindly concession he would have gained a life-friend and adherent. The Tory squire is, as a rule, much more advanced than the plutocrat. The penny local newspaper has an enormous circulation amongst them, but they don't read the political portion: no, it is the serial story that attracts them, and the Births, Deaths, and Marriages column.'

'They appreciate fiction then, Mr. Hardy? Do they read your stories about them with the same interest that Frank R. Stockton told me the Virginian negroes read his sketches of coloured life?'— 'Why, emphatically they are fond of fiction. They have far more romance and sentiment than the class above them, which has a struggle ever going on within its ranks for petty social superiority. This destroys all romance or capacity for romance.'

'Then the typical "Hodge," in your estimation, is non-existent, Mr. Hardy?'—'Certainly I have never met him. At close quarters no "Hodge" is to be seen, it is a delusion. Rustic ideas, the modes, the surroundings, appear retrogressive and unmeaning at first. After a time, if you live amongst them, variety takes the place of monotony. The people begin to differentiate themselves as in a chemical process. The labourer is disintegrated into a number of varied fellow-creatures, beings of many minds, infinite in difference: some happy, many serene, a few depressed, one here and there bright even to genius; some stupid, others wanton, others austere; some mutely Miltonic, some potentially Cromwellian. The men strong, heroic souls; the girls dainty heroines. One charming village girl the other day when I was complimenting her upon her good looks said, "Ah, but you don't think me so nice as Tess," mentioning one of my characters. I replied, "But she isn't real; you are." "What?" she cried, "oh, I thought she lived in that house over the hill there." She was much relieved that Tess was no practical rival.

'They are full of character, which is not to be found in the strained, calculating, unromantic middle classes; and for many reasons this is so. They are the representatives of antiquity. Many of these labourers about here bear corrupted Norman names; many are the descendants of the squires of the last century, and their faces even now strongly resemble the portraits in the old manorhouses. Many are, must be, the descendants of the Romans who lived here in great pomp and state for four hundred years. I have seen faces here that are the duplicates of those fine faces I saw at Fiesole, where also I picked up Roman coins the counterpart of those we find here so often. They even use Latin words here which have survived everything. As to my characters, Bathsheba Everdene and the Sergeant really lived, Shepherd Oak I knew well, and the Noble Dames are mostly drawn from life. The labourer as a rule is, as I depict him, rather fetishistic. Susan Nonsuch, in "The Return of the Native," still exists. In some parts the girls go out on Midsummer's Eve as they did in the "Woodlanders," in the hope of meeting him who will be their future husband. They are wonderfully good at description if you know their words, but it takes a lifetime to understand them, accent and turns of phrases mean so much with them. I have written now many years. My first attempt was a wild sort of manuscript, which fell into the hands of John Morley and George Meredith, who both strongly recommended me to take up fiction.'

The Art of Thomas Hardy, by Lionel Johnson, 1894
❡ Only two books on Hardy were published while he was still writing novels, both of them in 1894. One was an unimportant volume by Annie MacDonell, the other was Lionel Johnson's. This is an urbane, enthusiastic and (to modern taste) infuriatingly

digressive book. Johnson's view of Hardy does not differ much from that of other contemporaries: there is, for instance, the usual comparison between his rustics and those of Shakespeare, the usual praise of his sense of place and creation of the rural setting (all the extracts below relate to this). On at least two points, Johnson's views are less orthodox: his favourite Hardy novel is *The Return of the Native*, and he is very sympathetic to Hardy's view of life. He does not, however, like the more explicit statements of this view in *Tess*, and his objections to novels which, with 'insinuated argument', vindicate the ways of man to God lead one to guess that he must have liked Jude even less.

. . . And the plays are played out among the most appropriate scenes: be it woodland or moorland, sheepfold or dairy farm, sea-coast or inland, market town or hamlet, Mr. Hardy knows what the nature of things will bring about in each case. He has, what Hawthorne had, a gift of sight into the spirit of place: a most rare gift. With a few words, he makes us smell the damp woods; catch the change in the wind's voice, as it travels through each kind of tree; know the foldings of the hills by heart, and by instinct, what lies beyond them; recognize each tree, by the noise of its snapping twigs, or the rustle of its dead leaves underfoot; keep the path through the heath at night, by the feel of its worn herbage; remember, how the ash and the beech, more than other trees, hold the early dripping fog: a few words, and we can swear to the occupations of a dozen labourers, though in their Sunday dress, and without their implements; distinguish upon the road the farmer, whose negotiations at market have prospered, from him, who has not hit things off to his mind; is it not to be read in the complexion? As the naturalist with a bone, so Mr. Hardy with a word can construct for us the whole manner of a man, the whole aspect of a place. Not the looks of definite objects only, but their surrounding and inter-vening atmospheres, become plain to us; the blue mists, or dusty gold lights, or thin gray breaths of air: once familiarized with one of his places, we know all about it. If we step out of doors in Little Hintock, or upon Egdon, or at Casterbridge, in some dream or fancy of our own, we know our way; we know, according to season, what the wind will be doing with the cottage chimney smoke by nightfall, or what apples will be upon the grass by morning, or what prices are current at the corn exchange, or what likelihood there be of a fair lambing time. But if we search Mr. Hardy's books, to dis-cover why we know this so surely, we are hard put to it for a reason:

so delicate has been his manner, so natural and unobtrusive his 'mental tactility,' that we have learned it all from his pages, as we should learn it by experience: our certainty and familiarity have grown upon us. . . . Without the elaborate, slow pourtraiture of Egdon Heath, we should have missed some depths of tragedy in Eustacia, Yeobright, and his mother: without the detailed dairy work and field work of Tess, we should have missed the glow of her love, the strength of her endurance: the artist has felt the fulness of life, and made us feel it; with what force and what conviction, they best know, who best know Wessex. It is no small task, to set whole spheres of life and work in a light so true, that all must own its truth. Patience and loving study alone can do it: no brilliant epigram, nor biting phrase, can make us understand the slowly prevailing, gently lingering, charm of all those rural lives and ways. It is the province of a deeper art: an art, patient, studious, and sure: an art without those graces could but pourtray the country in its mean dulness, or in the violence of its incivility. 'In sleep,' writes Mr. Hardy, 'there come to the surface buried genealogical facts, ancestral curves, dead men's traits, which the mobility of daytime animation screens and overwhelms.' The 'sleep' of Wessex, its air of long repose, in which ancient memories assert their claims to life, is never far from Mr. Hardy's mind, when he dwells upon the present stir and business of Wessex: he writes of the labourers, who work there to-day; and the reader is left with thoughts of patriarchal days: from the faithful pourtraiture of a secluded village, a lonely farm, the reader gains that range and height of contemplation, whence the life of long and battling ages wears in part that look of still life, which it must wholly wear for eternal eyes. . . .

It is hard to express that singular quality of Mr. Hardy's writing, when he deals with the aspects of Wessex: that quality, by virtue of which the reader sees the very landscape in its exact truth: although Mr. Hardy is neither an 'impressionist,' nor a 'word-painter,' nor a maker of 'prose poems.' He has well recognised the part really played by the natural scenes of a landscape, in the daily life of those among them: he never makes the mistake of describing the scenery of his stories, as though it were fresh and new to his people. Few things are more curious, than the effect of trying to imagine, that the roads, the fields, the woods, familiar to us from childhood, are now seen by us for the first time: the landscape changes, and all is new, touched with fresh colours, seen under a strange light; the homeliness of the old place has gone. Most novelists are not at home among the places of their imagination:

from first to last, they describe their woods and fields, not as long familiarity makes them appear, but as they appear to unaccustomed eyes: there is no heart in them. But Mr. Hardy has the art of impressing upon us so strong a sense of familiarity with his scenes, that we read of Wessex, and we think of our own homes, far away and far different though they may be. . . .

In *The Woodlanders* and in *Tess of the D'Urbervilles*, Mr. Hardy avails himself, with admirable effect, of a peculiar mode in tenures: the system of 'liviers.' In the woodland story, Winterborne's tragic calamity in love, and heroism in death, are intensified, and in part occasioned, by his necessity of leaving his house: a necessity caused by the fall of an old man's frail life, brought about through his rustic superstition; and by the offended dignity of a capricious woman. In the later story, the final defeat of Tess is greatly assured by the same necessity, which casts her and her mother and her mother's children at the mercy of the world, leaving Tess to the temptation of helping them by a surrender to Alec D'Urberville. Interwoven thus with the fabric of the story, these facts of rural life quicken wonderfully our living interest: sudden death is a common device among the novelists: but the sudden deaths of old South and of poor 'Sir John,' involving plain, legal consequences of so tragic and pitiful an issue, are more moving than a score of less practical misfortunes. All the changes and chances of village life, migrations and depopulations; the terms of rural service, matters of fact about wage and hire; the variations in local prosperity, affairs of parchment and of record: all these become critical turns in a romance, at Mr. Hardy's bidding. . . .

The Quarterly Review, July 1901
From 'The Popular Novel'

. . . Mr Hardy's defects differ in their nature from Mr Meredith's, though, like certain of Mr Meredith's, they are due entirely to the limitations of his practical knowledge. His knowledge is sure and accurate as regards one class only. It is apt to fail him when he goes further: but of this class—the peasantry of the South of England—his knowledge is extraordinary; and it is allied with an insight into human nature which has enabled him to give a universal significance to characters and incidents which at first sight seem narrow in their marked provincialism. Here we have an example of the vision of real genius. Mr Hardy sees all the fundamental elements of the tragedy and the comedy of life, in the cottage,

11

and the dairy-farm, and the little country town, as clearly as others have seen them in palaces and in great cities; and his knowledge and grasp of what he thus sees is complete. Nor does he see only as an observer; he sees as a thinker also. In no English novelist, with the exception, perhaps, of George Eliot, is the quality of philosophic thought so remarkable as in Mr Hardy; but he never parades it. In him, as has been said of another writer, 'it is not apparent, except in the victories which it has won.' Only now and then do we see, by some direct indication, how constantly he has lived in the presence of all the deepest feelings which the old experience and the new knowledge of the world present to the human soul; and how closely, and with what sad irony, he has questioned 'the President of the Immortals' with regard to 'his sport with man.' Mr Hardy also, unlike Mr Meredith, possesses a style which is for his purpose perfect. Unlike Mr Meredith's, it never overshoots its mark. He has the clearness, the directness, the illuminated originality of vision which are characteristic of the great masters of his art. He is, in fact, within his own province, a master; and though locally and socially the limits of his province may seem narrow, the universalising quality of his genius has made this province a kingdom.

Such then, in respect of literary merit, being the position of Mr Meredith and Mr Hardy, how do they stand in respect of popularity? Of those living novelists whom we have already selected for notice as having achieved a popularity wide enough to make them representative of the condition of contemporary taste, Mr Meredith and Mr Hardy are those whose circle of readers is the smallest. Why is this the case? The reason cannot be that Mr Hardy and Mr Meredith are suffering from any accidental neglect—that they are not read because they happen to have escaped notice. They are read and admired by a minority quite sufficiently numerous to have forced them on the attention of the majority, had the majority been able to appreciate them. Nor again can they be unpopular because, like Mr Pater in his 'Marius,' they deal with aspects of life which only a few can understand, or which the many would turn away from as too serious for works of fiction. For in the first place, they deal with life as the ordinary man experiences it. In the second place, serious as their thought and intention is, no serious intellectual problems are ever obtruded by them on their readers; and in the third place, this discussion of serious problems by a novelist, even when obtruded in its least artistic form, is not itself any bar to popularity, as the case of Mrs Ward will show. . . .

[W. H. MALLOCK]

The Quarterly Review, April 1904

The Novels of Thomas Hardy
(on the publication of Macmillan's collected
edition of Hardy's novels in seventeen volumes)

... Thackeray, in the first portion of 'Vanity Fair,' and in some later works, effected a marked improvement in the art of novel-writing in England, in construction as well as in style; but to have definitely raised the standard of workmanship in this respect is one of the fine achievements of the author of 'The Return of the Native.' We think it is well to insist upon this, primarily, in attempting even a brief estimate of Mr Hardy's work as a novelist. For although the best writers of the younger generation have followed him in studying conciseness, arrangement, dramatic point, and, in a few instances, purity and expressiveness of style, yet, unfortunately, the average English work remains, not only pitifully inferior to the French, but inferior also in constructive art and vividness to the average American novel of the present day. Hence, as Mr Hardy complained some sixteen years ago, in a valuable essay on the reading of fiction, probably few general readers consider that to a masterpiece in story, no less than to a masterpiece in painting or sculpture, there appertains a beauty of shape capable of giving to the trained mind an equal pleasure.

Yet, no doubt, many persons, who did not care whether or not the English novel in Mr Hardy's hands had become a well-knit drama instead of the string of episodes which once it was, appreciated other splendid qualities in his rustic stories. First of all, he revealed to them the true romance of country life. He painted for them the woods, downs, meads, and heaths, where the Wessex labourer toiled, in a new and most impressive light. In that happy compromise between an essay in criticism and an anthology, 'Landscape in Poetry,' the late Professor Palgrave remarked in the literary treatment of natural scenery a general development. There was first a simple pleasure in describing single familiar objects; scenes were next lightly drawn as a background in the representation of human actions and manners. Then, as men gathered into cities for the business of life, and repaired to the country for pleasure and refreshment, a form of literature arose in which the loveliness and the benignity of the green earth were extolled. This idea of nature as a fair, beneficent power obtained in Wordworth's poetry its grandest and most complete expression; and, in an era of extraordinary industrial expansion, it has become one of the commonplaces of European letters.

It implies, however, a conception of the conditions of rustic existence which is not borne out by the experiences of the peasant himself. Not by residing in a thatched cottage, amid verdant fields circled by soft blue hills, does he become a poetic figure. The poetry of his mode of life consists in his having to work for his living in a dependence on the moods of sky, air, and earth, almost as absolute as is the dependence on the moods of sky, air, and water, of mariners in a lone sailing vessel on the high seas. Dawn and darkness, rain, wind, mist, and snow, the frost in winter, the summer drought—these, for him, are personal obstructors or assistants; and every hour of the day he must study and prepare for them. He does not always see in a sunset the beauty which Turner and Shelley have taught us to appreciate; he usually glances at it for another purpose, which Mr Hardy illustrates in the scene in 'The Woodlanders,' where the peasant girl Marty South is planting fir trees.

'She looked towards the western sky, which was now aglow like some vast foundry wherein new worlds were being cast. Across it the bare boughs of a tree stretched horizontally, revealing every twig against the evening fire, and showing in dark profile every beck and movement of three pheasants that were settling themselves down on it in a row to roost.

'"It will be fine to-morrow," said Marty, observing them with the vermilion light of the sun in the pupils of her eyes, "for they are a-croupied down nearly at the end of the bough. If it were going to be stormy they'd squeeze close to the trunk."'

This is excellent writing, inspired by knowledge and instinct with poetry; but a still finer and more complete revelation of the countryman's point of view is found in 'Far from the Madding Crowd,' where the shepherd, tending his lambing ewes on a winter's night upon the downs, pauses to glance at the sky.

'To persons standing alone on a hill during a clear midnight such as this, the roll of the world eastward is almost a palpable movement. The sensation may be caused by the panoramic glide of the stars past earthly objects, which is perceptible in a few minutes of stillness, or by the better outlook upon space that a hill affords, or by the wind, or by the solitude; but whatever be its origin, the impression of riding along is vivid and abiding. . . . The Dog-star and Aldebaran, pointing to the restless Pleiades, were half-way up the Southern sky, and between them hung Orion, which gorgeous constellation never burnt more vividly than now, as it swung itself forth above the rim of the landscape. Castor and Pollux, with their quiet shine, were almost on the meridian; the barren and gloomy Square of Pegasus was creeping round to the northwest; far away through the plantation, Vega sparkled like a lamp suspended amid the leafless trees, and Cassiopeia's chair stood daintily poised on the uppermost boughs.

'"One o'clock," said Gabriel.

'Being a man not without a frequent consciousness that there was some charm in this life he led, he stood still after looking at the sky as a useful instrument, and regarded it in an appreciative spirit, as a work of art superlatively beautiful.'

This shepherd is a type of the countryman described by Mr Hardy with the greatest sympathy. Mr Hardy's conception of the English peasant is somewhat partial, but most striking; and we fancy that such characters as Gabriel are depicted with the greatest sympathy because they clearly reflect a main idiosyncrasy of their author in noble conjunction with a higher quality of soul. They are supposed to unite the enervating fatalism that distinguishes Mr Hardy with a power of silent, grand endurance in adversity that a Roman Stoic would have admired. For instance, the scene in 'Far from the Madding Crowd,' from which we have just cited a passage, closes with a spectacle of disaster. The flock of ewes, representing Gabriel's savings after years of toil and thrift, and his prospect of acquiring a position of independence and comfort, are worried by a young dog into a chalk-pit, at the bottom of which he discovers them stretched all dying or dead. Misfortunes accumulate, as they often do in Mr Hardy's novels. Gabriel finds himself rejected by the woman he loves, poverty-stricken, and unable to obtain any sort of employment. Then, with that healthy disinclination to grieve over past sorrows, which amounts almost to temperamental cheerfulness in the generality of the English labouring classes, the shepherd goes in search of work.

'He had sunk from his modest elevation as pastoral king into the very slime-pits of Siddim; but there was left to him . . . that indifference to fate which, though it often makes a villain of a man, is the basis of his sublimity when it does not.'

Mr Hardy's heroes are all drawn on the same model. Gabriel Oak in 'Far from the Madding Crowd,' John Loveday in 'The Trumpet-Major,' Giles Winterborne in 'The Woodlanders,' are men of a similar nature. Michael Henchard in 'The Mayor of Casterbridge,' though lacking their inexpressible tenderness and purity of heart, is related to them in passive fortitude; and Clym Yeobright in 'The Return of the Native,' joins their family. A student and a sojourner in cities, he has, at first, a facility of expression, a radiant activity, and a resilience of mind, which exclude him from the company of Mr Hardy's heroes; but when he turns again for peace of soul to the rugged heath where he was born, he at last becomes as subdued in spirit as the strong rustic men who have been taught to go softly all their days, and to whom the sad art of renunciation is almost an instinct. Here, at least, Mr Hardy's poetic exaggeration of nature's utter sternness, as opposed to Wordsworth's equally poetic exaggeration of her benignity, leads to the conception of a fine type of character.

The disciplinary influence of country life supplies, indeed, one of those grandly constructive ideas which give to the Wessex novels their singular unity and consistency. It underlies the whole of the characterisation. While Mr Hardy's heroes are countrymen in whom the dumb passiveness of the peasantry under affliction rises into a moral grandeur of resignation, his men of the meaner sort are either townsmen or persons of urban culture. Manson, Sergeant Troy, Wildeve, Fitzpiers, D'Urberville, and some characters in the shorter tales, have many traits in common; and, through not having been chastened by a life of labour under natural conditions, they strangely resemble those women in Mr Hardy's novels who, belonging to the yeoman or better class, lead a sheltered, pleasant existence. Men and women, their characteristics can be given almost in the same words. They have somewhat of the moral poverty of children in that their reason and their propensities have no reciprocating influence; so they live on present emotions, and regard neither the past with understanding nor the future with circumspection. Though possessing as little real energy of resistance to fate as Mr Hardy's peasants, they have a buoyancy of spirit arising from the unrestrained sensibility which is the moving force of their lives; and, stimulated by whatever pleasing object chance places in their way, they are full of dangerous activity. The effect is that the men are refined sensualists and the women lighthearted coquets, who, in a search for personal admiration or fine shades of feeling, often become the victims of an overwhelming passion. Irresponsible, fascinating creatures, these 'children of a larger growth' are sometimes transfigured into incarnations of the tragic power of love, blind, disastrous, and ineluctable in its working. As wayward as fate itself, they invade, for some light whim, the settled lives of men whose calmness is but the equilibrium of great powers, and leave them terribly disordered. They are singularly apt to make the first advances; yet with all their eagerness for admiration they remain indifferent to the deep inarticulate devotion which they are at pains to excite. The tumult and not the depth of soul they approve, and thus they are won lightly by the voluble inconstant men whose failings they more innocently and weakly reflect. . . .   EDWARD WRIGHT

Notes on the Reviewers

ADAMS, FRANCIS (*Tess, Fortnightly Review*, 1 July 1892). 1862–93. Committed suicide after a short and stormy life. Spent some of his youth in Australia, where he worked for the *Sydney Bulletin*. Published *Leicester*, an autobiographical novel, 1884; *Tiberius*, a play (posthumous, 1894); and some poetry.

ALDEN, HENRY M. ('Thomas Hardy'—a note on *Jude, Harper's Weekly*, 8 December 1894). 1836–1919. After studying at Williams College and Andover Theological Seminary, Alden did a little teaching in New York and Boston before he began his life-long connection with Harper. He was managing editor of *Harper's Weekly*, 1863–9, and editor of *Harper's Magazine* from 1869 till his death. He was widely esteemed as an editor, and wrote a regular feature called 'The Editor's Study'. He published three books: *God in his World*, 1890; *A Study of Death*, 1895; *Magazine Writing and the New Literature*, 1908. In later years Alden tried without success to persuade Hardy to write his autobiography for Harper.

BROOME, SIR FREDERICK NAPIER (*Far from the Madding Crowd, The Times*, 25 January 1875). 1842–96. Colonial Governor. Sheep-farmer in New Zealand, 1857–69; Colonial Secretary of Natal, 1875, of Mauritius, 1880; Governor of Australia, 1882–90, of Barbados, 1890. Published some poetry, and was a frequent contributor to *The Times*.

ELLIS, HAVELOCK (*Jude, The Savoy*, October 1896). 1859–1939. Best known for his writings on sex, Havelock Ellis was also a literary critic and essayist. Taught in the bush in Australia as a young man, and much of his view of life arose out of the solitary thinking he did then. Studied medicine on his return to England, but never practised. He was the originator of the 'Mermaid series' of Elizabethan dramatists, and wrote many of the introductions. *Studies in the Psychology of Sex* appeared in six volumes, 1897–1910, and was later added to and revised. Among his many other books are *The Dance of Life*, 1923; *Impressions and Comments*, 3 vols., 1914–24; *My Life* (posthumous, 1940).

GILDER, JEANNETTE LEONARD ('Hardy the Degenerate' on *Jude, The World*, 13 November 1895). See also pp. 148–9. 1849–1916. Literary journalist and editor. Worked in Scribner's (under the editorship of her brother, Richard Watson Gilder) and wrote a number of columns in the New York *Herald*, including 'Chats about Books'. Helped to found *The Critic* in 1881, and edited it until it ceased independent publication in 1906. Wrote several plays, *The Autobiography of a Tomboy*, 1900, and *The Tomboy at Work*, 1904.

GOSSE, EDMUND (*Jude, Cosmopolis*, January 1896). 1849–1928. Began his career in the cataloguing section of the British Museum. His first publication was a volume of poems, and his collected poems came out in 1911. Translated Ibsen, and published *Studies in the Literatures of Northern Europe*, 1879. An accomplished linguist, he worked as translator to the Board of Trade after leaving the British Museum in 1875. Declined a professorship of English Literature at Harvard; was Clark lecturer at Trinity College, Cambridge, 1884–90. Librarian of the House of Lords, 1904–14. Made C.B., 1912, and knighted 1925. His most interesting book today is perhaps the autobiographical *Father and Son*, published anonymously in 1907, which tells of his upbringing among the Plymouth Brethren. Gosse saw himself as the English Sainte-Beuve, and was equally prolific—and often, perhaps, as lively.

HOW, WILLIAM WALSHAM (Letter to the *Yorkshire Post*, about *Jude*, 8 June 1896). 1823–97. First Bishop of Wakefield. It is unjust to Bishop How that he should be represented only by this ill-tempered letter, for he was a progressive and dedicated social worker, who devoted himself to welfare work in the East End of London, and was proud of his popular title of 'The Children's Bishop'; he also wrote on religious subjects.

HOWELLS, WILLIAM DEAN (*Jude, Harper's Weekly*, 7 December 1895). 1837–1920. One of the leading American novelists of his time, indigenous in subject-matter, realistic in method. *The Rise of Silas Lapham* (1885) is his best-known novel. He was editor of *The Atlantic Monthly* from 1872 to 1881 and a regular contributor to *Harper's* for some years after that, and from 1886 to 1891 took over the 'The Editor's Study' with a series of articles later collected as *Criticism and Fiction* (1891).

HUTTON, RICHARD HOLT (Most of Hardy's novels in *The Spectator*). 1826–97. Joint editor of *The Spectator*. Began life as a Unitarian, and intended to enter the ministry; after abandoning this intention, he edited *The Enquirer* (the Unitarian weekly), 1851–3, but his views were unacceptable to its readers. He later became an Anglican, with High Church, even Roman Catholic sympathies. In 1861, Meredith Townsend, who had just bought *The Spectator*, invited him to join as co-editor, with responsibility for the literary section; he held this post until his death. He always remained interested in theology, on which he wrote regularly. Published *Essays Theological and Literary* (1871) and several other works. Friend of Bagehot, F. D. Maurice, and Gladstone.

JAMES, HENRY (*Far from the Madding Crowd, The Nation*, 24 December 1874; letters to Stevenson about *Tess*, 19 March 1892, 17 February 1893). James' remarks on Hardy are possibly shrewd and certainly cutting; so, in fairness, we should offer some of Hardy's remarks on him. He called him 'Polonius of novelists', and wrote after reading *The Reverberator*: 'After this kind of work one feels inclined to be purposely careless in detail. The great novels of the future will certainly not concern themselves with the minutiae of manners ... James' subjects are those one could be interested in at moments when there is nothing larger to think of.'

JOHNSON, LIONEL (*The Art of Thomas Hardy*, 1894). 1867–1902. After leaving Oxford, went to London to follow a literary career, and reviewed for a number of papers. His poems were published in the first and second book of the Rhymers' Club; his first collection, entitled simply *Poems*, 1895; *Ireland and other poems*, 1897. Became a Roman Catholic in 1891. One of the leading *fin de siècle* poets, friendly with Yeats.

LANG, ANDREW (*Tess, New Review*, February 1892). 1844–1912. Journalist, poet, critic, historian. Perhaps best known for his translations of the *Odyssey* (with Butcher, 1879) and the *Iliad* (with Leaf and Myers, 1883); also wrote several books on Homer. Wrote on Scottish history, and was an early enthusiast for psychical research.

LE GALLIENNE, RICHARD (*Jude, The Idler*, February 1896). 1866–1947. Poet and essayist. Belonged to the Rhymers' Club, contributed to the *Yellow Book*, and wrote poetry typical of the nineties. Reviewed in *The Star* as 'Log-Roller' from 1891. As well as a great deal of verse, he published novels including *The Quest of the Golden Girl*, 1896; books of essays and travel, including *The Romantic Nineties*, 1890 and a paraphrase, 'from several literal translations', of the *Rubáiyát of Omar Khayyám*, 1897. Settled in U.S.A. in 1901 and later in France.

MALLOCK, WILLIAM HURRELL ('The Popular Novel' in the *Quarterly Review*, July 1901). 1849–1923. Author of novels, poems, religious and political works. *The New Republic* (1877) was a Platonic dialogue to demonstrate the impossibility of undogmatic belief. Other works included *The New Paul and Virginia*, or *Positivism on an Island*; *Is Life Worth Living?*; *The Old Order Changes* (his most popular novel); an attack on *Social Equality*; and a volume of Memoirs. Mallock became a Roman Catholic on his death-bed.

MEREDITH, GEORGE (Letters to Frederick Greenwood about *Tess*, 11 January, 23 February, 1892). 1828–1909. Meredith's friend Frederick Greenwood (1830–1909) was a Conservative journalist, editor of the *Cornhill* and then of the *Pall Mall Gazette*, which he helped to found. Meredith described himself as of the other persuasion politically but corresponded warmly with Greenwood on personal and literary matters.

MORLEY, JOHN, VISCOUNT MORLEY (Reader's report on *Under the Greenwood Tree*, September 1871). 1838–1923. Politician and author. Edited the *Fortnightly Review*, 1867–83; edited the English Men of Letters series from 1878; edited the *Pall Mall Gazette* from 1880. His political career followed after his literary one, and in 1883 he became Liberal MP for Newcastle-on-Tyne, and went on to hold office in the 1906 Liberal Government. His most ambitious work was his *Life of Gladstone*, 1903.

MORRIS, MOWBRAY ('Culture and Anarchy' in the *Quarterly Review*, April 1892). Presumably the same man who edited a number of English classics and wrote *Montrose* (English Men of Action series), *The First Afghan War*, and a very popular book on hunting with the Duke of Beaufort. He may have been the son of the Mowbray Morris who was the Manager of *The Times* from 1847 to 1873.

MOULE, HORACE (*Under the Greenwood Tree*, *Saturday Review*, 28 September 1872). (Died 24 September 1873.) Friend of Hardy's. Fellow of Queen's College, Cambridge. A Greek scholar, Moule is said to have advised Hardy to go on with his architectural studies rather than study Greek drama intensely. Published *Tempora Mutantur* (Essays, Verses, etc.), 1859; *Christian Oratory*, 1859; *The Roman Republic*, 1860; and was also a Poor Law inspector. He believed in Hardy's writing, and encouraged him constantly.

OLIPHANT, MRS MARGARET OLIPHANT ('The Anti-Marriage League' in *Blackwood's*, January 1896). 1828–97. Novelist. Her husband (who was also her cousin) died in 1859, leaving her with three children to bring up—besides her brother's children, for whom she assumed responsibility. Lived by writing, and brought out a constant stream of fiction and historical writing, much of it in *Blackwood's Magazine*. Her most famous work was the series of Chronicles of Carlingford (*Salem Chapel*, *The Rector and the Doctor's Family*, *The Perpetual Curate*, *Miss Marjoribanks*), serialised in *Blackwood's*, 1862–5: they were often taken for the work of George Eliot. Her autobiography was published posthumously, in 1899.

PICK, HARRY THURSTON (May have written the notice of *Jude* in the New York *Bookman*, January 1896), was the editor of *The Bookman*.

ROBINSON, EDWIN ARLINGTON (Sonnet 'For a Book by Thomas Hardy', *The Critic*, 23 November 1895). 1869–1935. This is the celebrated New England poet. Born in Maine, studied at Harvard, clerk in the New York Customs House for five years. Then a full-time writer until his death. Three times winner of the Pulitzer Prize. His first volume of poems, *The Torrent and the Night Before*, appeared in 1896, and his *Collected Poems* first appeared in 1921.

STEPHEN, SIR LESLIE (Letters to Hardy about *Far from the Madding Crowd*, 12 March, 13 April 1874). 1832–1904. Of Stephen's many scholarly works, the best known are *Hours in a Library* (mainly reprints of his contributions to the *Cornhill*), 1874–9, *History of English Thought in the Eighteenth Century*, 1876–81, *The Science of Ethics*, 1882, *An Agnostic's Apology*, 1893, *The English Utilitarians*, 1900. He was editor of the *Dictionary of National Biography* from 1882 to 1891; wrote several volumes in the English Men of Letters series; and contributed to many of the journals here represented, though we have not been able to trace his hand in any of the reviews of Hardy. The letters to Hardy were written in his capacity as editor of the *Cornhill*: he held this post from 1871 to 1882.

STEUART, JOHN A. (*Letters to Living Authors*, 1890). A prolific novelist, who continued to publish novels until 1927.

WATSON, SIR WILLIAM (*Tess*, *The Academy*, 6 February 1892). 1858–1935. Well known in his day as a poet: polished, Romantic, rather academic in style. Published twenty-eight volumes, mostly of poetry, and his collected poems appeared the year after his death. His most famous poem is probably 'Wordsworth's Grave'. Much of his work was on topical and political subjects: he opposed the Boer War, was admired by Gladstone, and is said to have been seriously considered as Poet Laureate in 1913, when Bridges was chosen. He is said to have forced the dismissal of Beardsley from the *Yellow Book*, by threatening to resign himself.

WRIGHT, EDWARD (On Thomas Hardy, *Quarterly Review*, April 1904). May be the same Edward Wright who edited Bacon's Essays and Marvell's poems in the *Little Library*.